Vincent Carruthers

FROGS
AND FROGGING

in Southern Africa

Struik Publishers (Pty) Ltd
(a division of New Holland Publishing
(South Africa) (Pty) Ltd)
Cornelis Struik House
80 McKenzie Street
Cape Town 8001
www.struik.co.za

First published in 2001

1 3 5 7 9 10 8 6 4 2

Publishing manager: Pippa Parker
Managing editor: Helen de Villiers
Editor: Helena Reid
Designer: Dominic Robson
Design Assistant: Illana Fridkin
Illustrator: Kerry Jenner
Cartographer: Carl Germishuys
Proofreader: Lindsay Norman
Indexer: Mary Lennox

Reproduction by Hirt & Carter (Pty) Ltd, Cape Town
Printed and bound by Creda Press (Pty) Ltd

ISBN 1 86872 607 X

Cover: Rattling Frog and illustrations of Painted Reed Frogs
Back cover: Southern Ghost Frog
and illustrations of Painted Reed Frogs
Title page: Marsh Frog
Page 5: Banded Rubber Frog emerging from log (Les Minter)

CONTENTS

ACKNOWLEDGEMENTS

Frogs and Frogging in Southern Africa is the child of a more formal book, *South African Frogs*, written by Neville Passmore and myself and first published more than twenty years ago. Evidence of that parentage will be found throughout the following pages. Dr Passmore's science and scholarship earned a high reputation for *South African Frogs* and it has become the standard work in the field. I am extremely grateful to him for allowing me to re-use so much of his original work in this new publication.

The compact disc that accompanies this book has been compiled from an earlier CD, *South African Frog Calls*, produced by Megatone Studios. I acknowledge with thanks Neville Passmore's and Jürgen Zähringer's permission to re-use those recordings. The authors of the recordings are acknowledged on the disc.

Other friends and colleagues have also provided valuable assistance. I am most grateful to Dr Les Minter, Marius Burger, Richard Boycott, James Harrison, Professor Alan Channing and particularly my wife, Dr Jane Carruthers, who generously gave their expertise, their time, their photographs and their encouragement to this venture.

I have made use of a wide range of published texts. In a book of this size it is not possible to list all of these references in full, but I acknowledge with thanks the work of the following authors in their specialized fields:

Taxonomy and distribution: Avian Demography Unit, UCT, JP Bogart, Richard Boycott, Alan Channing, John Comrie, Greig A Dawood, Atherton de Villiers, Alice Grandison, D Hendricks, JD Jurgens, Angelo Lambiris, Charles Parry, Martin Pickersgill, John Poynton, Lyn Raw, CT Stuart, John Visser

Breeding and behaviour: Patricia Backwell, BI Balinsky, R Cavill, Alan Channing, Louis du Preez, CE Gow, Dawid Kok, Les Minter, Guy Palmer, Charles Parry, Neville Passmore, MT Seaman, Arne Schiotz, Steve Telford, DE van Dijk, John Visser, Vincent Wager

Palaeontology: JM Anderson, Robert Carrol, Colin MacRae, Greg Retallack

Toxicology: A Leisewitz, TW Naude, Harrison Ndlovo, Leron Pantonowitz

Vincent Carruthers
April 2001

INTRODUCTION TO FROGGING

Going frogging

Frogging is not just about frogs. It is about exploring wetlands, listening to the sounds of an African night, observing and conserving the natural world. Frogging can be science or it can be recreation. To some it means researching for a Ph.D., to others it means exciting discoveries on a summer holiday. Many may simply go frogging through the pages of this book.

The first part of the book introduces frogs and aspects of their biology, and then discusses habitats and the ways in which they influence frog behaviour. Chapters are arranged according to five basic southern African biomes (major ecological communities characterized by a dominant vegetation) – savanna, grassland, forest, fynbos and desert. Each chapter is then sub-divided into the main frog habitats found within that biome. Frogs that commonly breed in each habitat are listed, and examples of interesting adaptations and behaviour are discussed. Many frogs are found in more than one habitat and therefore appear on several lists. It is hoped that this will assist froggers in knowing where to look and what to expect.

The second part of this book describes and illustrates southern Africa's nearly 130 frog species, to facilitate identification in the field.

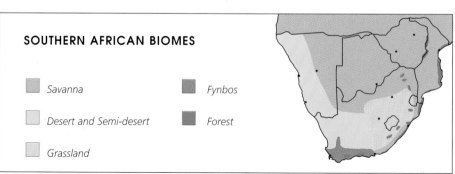

SOUTHERN AFRICAN BIOMES

- Savanna
- Desert and Semi-desert
- Grassland
- Fynbos
- Forest

Names and terms

Scientific names of frogs indicate the zoological classification of the species and are subject to rigorous international rules. They comprise two or, occasionally, three, Latinized words describing a characteristic of the frog, its locality, the person who is honoured for its discovery, or a similar association. The first word refers to the genus to which the frog belongs, the second indicates the species and a third word may be added to indicate a subspecies. Scientific names at genus and species level are always italicized with only the first word beginning with a capital letter.

Common names are usually easier to remember, but there is no standardization and different names are sometimes used by different people. English common names have been used for all species covered by this book. They follow those that were published in the standard work, *South African Frogs*, and are the names most widely accepted. Technical terms have been used as little as possible and terms that may be unfamiliar are explained in the glossary on page 93.

FROGS – THEIR PLACE IN THE ANIMAL KINGDOM

Animals are classified into a hierarchy of categories based on skeletal or other features that indicate a common evolutionary ancestor.

Phylum	The animal kingdom is divided into 25 phyla. Frogs belong to the phylum **Chordata** or **vertebrates** – animals with a backbone.
Class	There are five classes of vertebrates: fish, amphibians, reptiles, birds and mammals. Frogs are **amphibians** – a class of vertebrate animals with two phases to their lives: the tadpole and the four-legged adult (amphi = two, bios = life).
Order	Amphibians are divided into three orders. Frogs are tail-less amphibians and belong to the order **Anura** (a = absent, ura = tail) or **batrachians**. Batrachians are found on all continents except Antarctica. The other two orders are the Caudata, salamanders and newts from the northern hemisphere, and the Apoda, worm-like caecilians from equatorial rain forests.
Family	There are 18 families of frogs in the world, nine of which occur in southern Africa.
Genus	There are about 270 genera worldwide and 33 in southern Africa.
Species	There are about 2 500 species worldwide and about 130 in southern Africa.
Subspecies	Sometimes a population of frogs is separated from others of its species by a barrier such as a mountain or desert. If these isolated frogs show consistent differences from the rest of the species, but could still breed with them if the barrier were removed, then they can be considered to be a subspecies.

Painted Reed Frog

Finding and observing frogs

With a few exceptions, frogs are nocturnal or crepuscular animals and they can best be found by tracking their calls after dark. All that is needed is a reliable torch and a good deal of patience, but they are not always easy to locate, even when calling. They usually remain well concealed and calls sometimes seem to be ventriloquial. In such circumstances it is advisable to work with one or more partners positioned well apart. Each person points a torch in the direction of the sound. The place where the torch beams intersect becomes the focal point of the hunt. Approach the call site slowly and keep the direct torchlight off the frogs. If they are disturbed and stop calling, freeze instantly, switch off the torches and remain motionless until calling starts up again, otherwise the frogs will quickly slip away.

Frog calls

Frogs are more often heard than seen, and utter a number of calls – **mating, territorial, release** and **distress** calls. Of these, mating calls are most commonly heard, made by males to attract females to the breeding site. The mating call is unique to each species and the hearing of the female is attuned so that she is responsive only to that call.

FROGGING PRECAUTIONS

Many wetlands in southern Africa are contaminated with bilharzia. Reduce contact with the water by wearing wellington boots or anglers' waders. Even with such protection, getting wet while frogging is inevitable and when it happens, dry any wet skin vigorously and without delay.

Malaria is an even more serious threat, especially when frogging in low-lying areas. Always take medically recommended prophylactics and use mosquito repellant, remembering that a mosquito proboscis can penetrate thin clothing. Have a medical check if you have been exposed to malaria or bilharzia as both diseases are far less serious if diagnosed early.

In wildlife sanctuaries be mindful of other inhabitants of wetlands such as crocodiles (below) and hippos and in urban environments beware of human predators that lurk in lonely places at night.

Paired vocal sacs of a Grass Frog vibrate to give a trill like a referee's whistle.

The fragile vocal sac of a Reed Frog has a disc of thicker skin that covers it when collapsed.

The large-chambered vocal sac of the Giant Bullfrog creates a deep booming sound.

Calling, and thus mating, is stimulated by different factors in different species. Rain is the most common stimulant and some species, Squeakers, for example, immediately react to any precipitation. Other species, such as Bullfrogs, require temporary rain pools to be filled for breeding so they wait for four or five consecutive days of rain before they start calling. Increased temperature is another stimulant and many of the toads start calling with the warmer spring evenings. Because temperature increases usually precede the advent of rains in the summer rainfall areas, toads are sometimes credited with the ability to predict rain.

Mating calls summon females from afar and some species form choruses to give the approaching females a larger and louder 'target area' to locate. Choruses are well organized even if they sound chaotic to a human listener. Two close neighbours within a chorus alternate their calling to avoid mutual interference. In choruses of Kassinas, Rain Frogs and other species, one caller triggers an immediate response from his neighbour who triggers another, and so on – a kind of batrachian Mexican wave.

The volume of sound generated by such small animals is astonishing. It is achieved by passing air over the vocal chords and letting it resonate in an expanded vocal sac under the throat. The air is not exhaled while calling but passes back and forth between the lungs and vocal sac. The shape of the vocal sac in different species varies considerably.

The mating call is the way frogs identify one another and it is therefore the most reliable way for us to identify species. Scientists are increasingly using the analysis of frog sounds to resolve questions of taxonomy.

The position from which a male chooses to call is important and he will defend it against any competitor by uttering a special **territorial call**. If that fails he may attack the intruder, pushing with his expanded vocal sac, wrestling or kicking.

In the sexual frenzy at the breeding site males sometimes inadvertently clasp other males which then emit a sharp rebuff in the form of a **release call** that usually solves the problem. Females also give a release call to terminate mating.

Another component in the frog vocabulary is the **distress call** given by either sex if they are seized by a predator.

Reproduction and development

Once females are attracted to the breeding site, mating takes place. Fertilization is external and the male, which is usually smaller than the female, clasps his mate in amplexus and deposits sperm onto the eggs as they are laid. The eggs are laid in positions where they will be protected as far as possible from predators, bacteria and a fickle climate. The various ways in which southern African frogs overcome the vulnerability of their eggs are discussed in the pages ahead.

Metamorphosis

After a period of several days the eggs hatch into tadpoles. The principal distinction be-tween frogs and other vertebrate animals is their two-part life – the juvenile tadpole and the adult quadruped. Metamorphosis – the transition from one stage to the other – is a remarkable biological process.

Red Toads laying strings of eggs.

The tadpole is usually aquatic, obtaining oxygen through gills and feeding on algae and other organic matter in the water. In species that do not breed in water, the tadpole is sup-ported in a fluid jelly and feeds off the egg yolk. Metamorphosis is driven by the release of hor-mones from the thyroid and pituitary glands in the tadpole. Within a few days the tail, fins, gills and specialized mouthparts that equipped it for life in water are lost. Internal organs change, as herbivorous digestion makes way for a new carnivorous habit; and the excretary sys-tem switches from processing ammonia to urea. A full vertebrate skeleton and muscle system develops together with tongue, eyelids and a totally different type of skin.

Respiration and the skin

The skin of a frog differs from that of other ver-tebrates in a number of ways. It is permeable to water so that, if unprotected in dry conditions, the frog soon desiccates. Most frogs therefore retreat into protective, humid places during the heat of the day. Some species, however, are capable of altering the pigmentation in the skin so that it becomes whitish and reflects heat, allowing the frogs to remain in open sunlight.

The skin also absorbs oxygen and this allows frogs to remain underwater for long periods of time. Frogs do not have a diaphragm muscle to inhale air as we do. Instead, air is pumped into the lungs by continuous movement of the throat that can easily be seen when they are at rest.

Bullfrog in the process of metamorphosis.

Glands in the skin secrete fluids, which serve a number of purposes: some keep the skin moist to allow oxygen absorption, others are toxic or distasteful and help to defend the frog against predators.

Distribution

Frogs occur throughout southern Africa, even in the Namib desert. A number of factors influence their distribution but, because of their porous skin, they generally prosper in localities that are warm and damp. The greatest number of species can therefore be found in the eastern regions where high rainfall combines with warm year-round temperatures. For example, 41 frog species are found in the tropical climate of St Lucia, whereas only five occur in the dry, arid conditions around Springbok.

Some species have extremely limited ranges, such as the Table Mountain Ghost Frog and Amatola Toad, while others are widely dispersed in a variety of localities and climatic regions. However, most species are fairly restricted in the type of habitat they prefer, especially in their choice of breeding site.

Feeding

Frogs normally take live prey and swallow it whole. In all southern African species (except the Platanna which feeds under water and has no tongue) the tongue is fixed to the front of the mouth and flipped forward and out to pick up food items. The diet usually consists of insects and other invertebrates. Most species have no teeth although some have rudimentary tooth-like structures in the roof of the mouth. Bullfrogs have serrations in the upper jaw and two projections in the lower jaw with which they hold onto prey such as mice, fledgling birds, large insects and other frogs.

Tooth-like projections are visible in the jaw of a Bullfrog.

Frogs fall prey to a number of predators, the common ones being birds, snakes and carnivorous mammals, but even creatures like spiders and insects feed on the smaller species.

Giant Bullfrog eating a Red Toad.

Les Minter

Fishing Spider consuming a Waterlily Reed Frog.

Eyes and ears

With the exception of some of the burrowing species, the eyes are large and well developed for nocturnal activity. The tympanum, or eardrum, of a frog is also usually large and conspicuous because calling – and therefore hearing – is of considerable importance, as this is the manner in which males and females get together to breed. As a general rule, the lower the pitch of the call, the larger the diameter of the tympanum.

FROGS AND TOADS

The terms 'frog' and 'toad' originated centuries ago in Britain where only two genera occur naturally, *Bufo* (toads) and *Rana* (frogs). As knowledge of world zoology expanded, the terms were applied loosely to a range of unrelated amphibians – the only criteria appear to be whether the animal was likeable (frog) or loathsome (toad).

More recently, and sensibly, 'toad' has been used for members of the Bufonid family (which includes several genera) and other words such as 'treefrog', 'squeaker', etc. have been used for the other families or genera. 'Frog' is now used to denote all families of tail-less amphibians, including toads. The toad family generally lay their eggs in strings in the water and they usually have large parotid glands behind their eyes. Other families of frogs each have their own distinctive characteristics. This is how the terms are used in this book.

Eastern Olive Toad in full cry.

PART ONE

SAVANNA: BUSHVELD AND LOWVELD

A savanna pan may have several distinctly different habitat zones each with its particular range of frogs.

Much of Africa south of the equator comprises vast stretches of open woodland interspersed with an under-storey of grass. This is the African savanna, best known for big game, but also an area rich in frog life. The savanna spreads from arid Namibia across the bushveld plateau of Botswana and Zimbabwe and down into the coastal lowveld. It is a summer rainfall area receiving an average of about 300 mm per annum in the west and well over 1 000 mm on the east coast. Because of these climatic differences few frog species are distributed evenly throughout this whole region. Some are tropical species found mainly in the north while others are specially adapted for the drier conditions in the west. But the greatest diversity of species is concentrated in the lowveld that extends from the Mozambique plains south along the coast of KwaZulu-Natal and up the Limpopo and Zambezi valleys. Here the combination of high rainfall, temperatures and humidity is particularly conducive to frog life.

Large river systems drain the bushveld hinterland and temporary or semi-permanent pans collect the summer showers in the flatter areas. It is around these pans that most frogs gather to breed. The character of pans differs substantially in different parts of the savanna. In the west they are shallow and typically circular with muddy banks exposed by the fluctuating water-level. In the wetter east the pans are surrounded by dense stands of reeds, inundated grass and copses of trees. At the peak of the rainy season in the lowveld it is not exceptional to find up to twenty species of frogs breeding in a single pan. Competition for call sites under

Savanna

such circumstances results in different species occupying different zones of the pan to reduce congestion – some species will call from the mud-banks, others from the grass, the reeds, the trees or out in the open water. Each of these zones can be studied as a distinct habitat with its own particular range of species.

The banks of pans

Species to look for:

Banded Rubber Frog 54	Tremolo Sand Frog 72	Knocking Sand Frog 72
Natal Sand Frog 73	Tandy's Sand Frog 72	Beaded Sand Frog 72
Spotted Shovel-nosed Frog 60	Mottled Shovel-nosed Frog 60	Guinea Shovel-nosed Frog 60
Eastern Olive Toad 76	Guttural Toad 75	Kavanga Pygmy Toad 77
Western Olive Toad 76	Ornate Frog 71	Darling's Golden-backed Frog 82

From partially concealed positions on the edges of pans, the high-pitched 'pirrrrrr' of **Banded Rubber Frog** males can be heard over long distances on still nights. While the call of every frog is unique to the species, few are as distinctive as this call. During the day, these frogs take refuge in hollow logs, several of them often climbing into the same cavity.

The striking red, black and white colours are aposematic, signifying to would-be predators that the frog is poisonous (see box on page 21). Another defence mechanism of this frog is to stand very tall on its spindly legs, giving the impression that it is larger than it really is. It is unable to leap and is more inclined to walk or run. Banded Rubber Frogs are unusual in that they readily eat ants, evidently impervious to the formic acid that deters most other species.

The different species of Sand Frogs are similar in size and general appearance. The **Tremolo Sand Frog** and the **Knocking Sand Frog** are particularly difficult to tell apart and they often call together in choruses on the banks of pans and vleis. For many years these two very common species were thought to be one. It was only when they were heard, not merely seen together that their totally different calls revealed two separate species. **Tandy's Sand Frog** from the scrub and grasslands of the Eastern Cape was similarly identified as late as 1994. Apart from its call, and differences in DNA, it is indistinguishable from the Tremolo Sand Frog of the savanna and the **Cape Sand Frog** of the fynbos.

Sand Frogs have hard, calloused tubercles on each heel and they use these to shuffle backwards into the soil, corkscrewing slowly around as they burrow.

The poisonous Banded Rubber Frog elevating itself to deter predators.

The head-first burrowing technique of the Shovel-nosed Frog.

Quite a different method of digging is used by the **Shovel-nosed Frogs**. They have hard, sharp, wedge-shaped snouts with which they push their way into the soil. To facilitate tunnelling head first they have small eyes and a pointed skull with an undershot jaw. The method of digging is efficient and they disappear underground far more rapidly than the Sand Frogs. They call from inside their burrows, an incessant buzzing, and the eggs are laid in a rubbery mass in an underground chamber in the muddy banks. The female remains with the eggs and once the tadpoles start to hatch she digs a tunnel to the water's edge. The tadpoles wriggle onto the back of the female and she transports them down the tunnel to the water where they complete their development.

A common sound on a summer evening in the bushveld is the quacking bray of the **Eastern Olive Toad**. Slight differences in the call and colouration of specimens from the drier, western region have led zoologists to regard them as a different species – **Western Olive Toad** – but the difference in call is difficult to detect without electronic instruments.

Open water

Species to look for:

Red Toad 77	Red-legged Kassina 57	African Bullfrog 70
Giant Bullfrog 70	Common Platanna 53	Tropical Platanna 53

Red Toad calling while floating.

All southern African toads lay their eggs in strings in water but in most cases calling and initial courtship takes place on land. The **Red Toad**, however, calls while floating in open water. The call is easily recognizable: a long, deep 'whoooomp' that is kept up day and night during overcast weather. The sonorous tone is achieved by an enormous vocal sac that engulfs throat, chest and arms, and the floating frog pitches fore and aft as air passes between the lungs and vocal sac. Red Toads are also common around human dwellings and readily breed in dams, tanks, swimming pools or other man-made water bodies. When not breeding, they forage long distances

Savanna

A Red Toad is revealed in its refuge under the bark of a willow tree.

Red-legged Kassina supporting itself on vegetation while calling in deep water.

from water and they climb trees or rough-plastered walls to find a safe retreat. Red Toad tadpoles are readily identified because they swarm in dense, football-sized groups several centimetres below the surface. A constant column of tadpoles commutes between the main swarm and the surface to aerate their gills. Another caller from out in open water is the **Red-legged Kassina**. It does not float while calling, but clutches onto water plants, keeping most of the body submerged. The noisy clucking call can often be heard in pans in the coastal lowveld, but the frogs quickly duck underwater if approached, and sightings are uncommon.

Inundated grass

Species to look for:

Natal Leaf-folding Frog 58	Snoring Leaf-folding Frog 58	Golden Leaf-folding Frog 58
Delicate Leaf-folding Frog 58	Knysna Leaf-folding Frog 58	Greater Leaf-folding Frog 57
Dwarf Grass Frog 83	Speckled-bellied Grass Frog 82	Uzungwa Grass Frog 83
Mascarene Grass Frog 83	Broad-banded Grass Frog 83	Striped Grass Frog 83
Guibe's Grass Frog 84	Sharp-nosed Grass Frog 82	Plain Grass Frog 82
Snoring Puddle Frog 89	East African Puddle Frog 89	Bubbling Kassina 61
Common Caco 88		

After good rains the grass around the perimeters of pans is inundated with shallow water. This is the favoured breeding site of **Leaf-folding Frogs**. Egg predation is a serious threat in a lowveld pan and Leaf-folding Frogs have an extraordinary method of protecting their eggs. Calling males attract females to the elongated grass leaves. While mating, the pair moves slowly along the length of a partially submerged leaf and, as eggs are laid, the male fertilizes them and folds and seals the leaf into a tube around them. The leaf-tube is glued together with the adhesive fluids secreted by the female. The eggs develop safely within the tube and as the tadpoles hatch the glue softens and they are released.

Male Leaf-folding Frogs protect their call sites from other males by giving a buzzing spacing call. However, smaller, pirate males often lie quietly close by and when a female is attracted by the call, the smaller frog intercepts and mates with her.

Leaf-folding Frogs laying eggs and enclosing them in a leaf-tube.

Grass Frogs also breed in shallow, flooded grassland where their camouflage and secretive habits conceal them well. They have powerful hind legs and can leap extraordinary distances to escape and disappear under cover. The longest recorded frog jump in the world is credited to the **Sharp-nosed Grass Frog** (see box on page 22).

Grass Frogs are among the best examples of how individual callers avoid confusion by separating their calls with split-second precision. Each individual makes his call during the brief interval between the calls of his neighbour. Spacing themselves out among the shallow grassland, each frog is clearly audible, even though the total chorus sounds chaotic.

Frogs also divide up the calling hours of the night to avoid congestion. **Puddle Frogs** and **Bubbling Kassinas** are the first to call, sometimes starting during the mid-afternoon. At dusk the **Cacos** begin and later the **Broad-banded Grass Frog.** As the Puddle Frog calls fade away in the early part of the night the screeching of **Plain Grass Frog** becomes dominant. The **Sharp-nosed Grass Frog** is usually the last to start and finish, continuing to call until after midnight.

Reed-beds

Species to look for:

Pickersgill's Reed Frog 63	Tinker Reed Frog 65	Waterlily Reed Frog 65
Long Reed Frog 63	Argus Reed Frog 63	Painted Reed Frog 64

The pans and vleis of the lowveld frequently have beds of tall reeds at the edges where colourful Reed Frogs are to be found. Among the best known in this group are the beautiful **Painted Reed Frogs**, which are found throughout sub-Saharan Africa in many different colour forms. An indication of the variability in pattern is shown in the field guide section on the distribution map on page 64.

Colour is also used for defence: several species of Reed Frogs flash the brightly coloured inner surfaces of their limbs when they jump, thus confusing pursuers when the colour disappears on landing. Painted Reed Frogs can be heard in almost every reed-fringed pan within

Savanna

A lowveld pan with reeds and inundated grass.

their range. The males climb up the reed stems to call and their piping whistles, often in large choruses, carry long distances. The call site is strongly defended. Should another male come too close, the normal mating call is replaced by a threatening screech. If that has no effect, the contestants try to kick each other from the reed stem until one or other retreats.

Each species of Reed Frog has a different method of protecting its eggs. The translucent green **Waterlily Reed Frog** lays its eggs in a layer between overlapping waterlily pads or other flat leaves that are then glued together by the adhesive egg jelly. To attract a mate to the right locality the males call from waterlily pads or other vegetation at water-level.

The **Argus Reed Frog** also calls from positions near the surface of the water and deposits its eggs in small clusters on submerged vegetation.

In the case of the rare **Pickersgill's Reed Frog** the eggs are laid in a jelly mass on vegetation just above water-level. As they develop the jelly softens and the tadpoles slip into the water. The **Tinker Reed Frog** lays its eggs in a similar manner. It gets its name from the call – a sharp, double 'tap, tap' as if made by a small hammer on metal.

The inner limb of the Painted Reed Frog flashes for a moment as it jumps – then disappears.

A Painted Reed Frog dislodges a challenger from its call site.

TYPES OF WETLAND

Wetland scene

A variety of words are used to describe wetland localities. Many of these are peculiarly South African, others have been imported and have acquired slightly different interpretations in the move. This book uses the following terms to describe different frog habitats:

Pan: A depression filled by rainwater and depleted by evaporation or absorption into the substrate, i.e. not fed, nor drained, by a watercourse. Pans vary in size from many hectares to a few square metres. They may hold water for some time after rains but they are seldom permanent and they have widely fluctuating water-levels. Water-loving grasses, sedges and other aquatic plants are usually associated with pans. The banks may include open mud, inundated grass, reed-beds or copses of overhanging trees – all of which attract different species of frogs.

Pool: A small, sometimes man-made depression such as a ditch or vehicle track filled with rainwater. Water retention is short but successive rains may keep a pool filled for several months, thus allowing frogs to breed. Plants inundated by, or associated with pools are generally not specialized, water-loving species. Animal life (and hence predators) in the pool is limited.

Flood-plain pan: A depression along a river-bank that retains flood water after the river has receded.

Lake: A large, natural body of fresh water such as Lake Chrissie or Lake Sibaya. Lakes support relatively few breeding populations of frogs because of wave action and the presence of predators.

Dam: A man-made impoundment of the flow of a watercourse. Most dams are used for irrigation or for watering livestock, and can support specialized aquatic vegetation and animal life. Frogs usually breed in the headwaters of the dam or along shallow parts of the bank. A distinction is drawn between dams and large irrigation or hydro-electric schemes such as the Gariep Dam or Hartbeespoort Dam. These do not attract many frogs for the same reasons as lakes do not attract them.

Pond: A small, permanent body of standing water. Natural ponds are uncommon in southern Africa except in high rainfall areas where they are sheltered from evaporation by forests or deep embankments. Most ponds are ornamental or agricultural. Certain species are attracted to ponds and sometimes assemble in large numbers to breed.

Vlei: Part of a watercourse where it spreads out over a flat valley forming a marshy wetland with inundated grass, sedges, reeds and other specialized water-loving vegetation. Vleis usually dry up partly or entirely during the dry season. They are the breeding ground for many different species.

In the Western Cape, the term vlei is used for water bodies that are called pans or lakes elsewhere, e.g. Rondevlei.

The small secondary vocal sacs of the Waterlily Reed Frog are used as miniature fists to punch competitive males.

Argus Frog calling from reeds just above the surface of the water.

Trees

Species to look for:

Foam Nest Frog 65   Brown-backed Tree Frog 59

During the rainy season one frequently finds balls of white foam suspended on branches over water. These are the ingenious nests of the **Foam Nest Frog**. Before laying her eggs the mating female secretes a fluid which is churned into a stiff froth by continuous movement of the hind legs of the mating pair. They are joined by several other males who jostle for positions close to the female. After about 15 minutes the female releases the first batch of eggs and they are fertilized by her mating partner as well as the other males nearby. As the eggs are laid, all of the frogs churn them into the foam. The process lasts all night with the female periodically leaving the nest to re-hydrate herself in the water below and frequently changing partners on her return. The following night she sometimes returns alone to add more foam to the outside of the nest. In sunlight the outer surface of the nest hardens into a crust. The foam protects the eggs from aquatic predators and functions as an insulator, allowing the eggs to develop at an even temperature. Birds and other predators occasionally plunder the nest in times of severe food shortage but under normal conditions the effort required to find a tiny egg in the

Foam Nest Frog nests in branches overhanging a pan.

A group of Foam Nest Frogs creating a nest.

POISONOUS FROGS . . .

Many frogs secrete toxic substances from their skin to deter predators. Toads have large parotid glands on the neck and these release a distasteful whitish fluid when the animal is molested. Dogs froth at the mouth after mouthing a toad. To avoid these effects a mongoose eats a toad from the underside, leaving the upper, glandular skin untouched. The secretion is cardiotoxic and causes hallucinations and heart failure in humans if absorbed in sufficient quantity. It does not, however, cause warts. Platannas exude a slippery mucous making them difficult to hold. It is also poisonous and when a heron or kingfisher catches a Platanna it has to thrash and scrape away this fluid before swallowing the frog.

The adhesive secretion of Rain Frogs is also toxic and is discharged copiously when they are threatened. The local name for the Desert Rain Frog is 'melk padda' (milk frog) because of the white fluid it exudes when molested. The Banded Rubber Frog releases a particularly potent toxin from its glossy skin. The black, red and white colouring is a warning to predators. Handling this frog can cause a rash on sensitive skin. In one recorded case where the handler had abrasions on his hands, symptoms included contractions of the chest, respiratory difficulty, loss of balance and nausea. In another instance a ten-year-old boy handled a Banded Rubber Frog and half an hour after releasing it, he inadvertently rubbed his eyes and immediately suffered excruciating pain. After rinsing with milk (the only liquid readily available), the pain subsided with no long term effects. It is important to remember that frogs cannot administer venom themselves and contamination can be prevented by avoiding contact with the eyes, nose, mouth and open wounds.

. . . AND MEDICINAL FROGS

Despite their toxic secretions (or because of them) frogs are commonly used in traditional food and medicine. In the Northern Province, Botswana and Mozambique Giant Bullfrogs and African Bullfrogs are fried and eaten, the legs and webbing being particularly favoured. In Zulu traditional medicine, burnt frogs are mixed with herbs in the treatment of asthma and chronic oedema. Small quantities of toad skin are administered to treat irregular heartbeat, the cardiotoxins having an effect similar to digitalis.

Medieval English medical practice had a wide range of uses for frogs: a live frog in the mouth cured an inflamed throat and, if swallowed, would cure incontinence. Frog soup made from nine frogs was just the thing for whooping cough and the legs of frogs dangled around the neck healed scrofula. Eye diseases were cured by someone first licking the eye of a frog and then licking the eye of the patient. Nosebleeds, earache and sprained ankles all had frog-based remedies and tonsillitis could be prevented by wearing a string from which a toad had been hanged until dead.

A Banded Rubber Frog.

mass of inedible foam seems to deter potential raiders. After about five days the developing tadpoles work their way to the bottom of the nest. They break through the crust and drop into the water below where they complete their metamorphosis. Another savanna tree frog, the **Brown-backed Tree Frog** is found only in the lowveld region. Males call from exposed positions high in the branches of trees near water and are easy to pick out in torchlight. By day they bury themselves by digging into the soil and eggs are believed to be laid underground.

FROG ATHLETICS

It began in 1867 with Mark Twain's delightful story, *The Celebrated Jumping Frog of Calaveras County*. Now, every May, Angel's Camp, Calaveras County in California hosts the County Fair and Jumping Frog Jubilee, complete with fast food stalls, brass bands and beauty contests. Frogs compete under strict rules for the longest distance covered in three consecutive jumps. The current record is 6,6 metres. It was set in 1986 by a 16 cm American Bullfrog called 'Rosie the Ribiter' and is blithely called a 'world record' by the Americans. The real world record, listed in the Guinness Book of Records, is 10,3 metres and is held by a South African Sharp-nosed Grass Frog. The athletic prowess of Grass Frogs was first harnessed by Dr Walter Rose, author of the informative book, *The Reptiles and Amphibians of Southern Africa*. At a charity fete in Cape Town in 1953 his entrant, especially imported from Zululand, outclassed the local Cape River Frogs and covered 9,9 m in three jumps.

Two years later, a Sharp-nosed Grass Frog was sent to the United States to compete in the famous Jumping Frog Jubilee. How the spectators laughed at this little 5 cm South African competing against bullfrogs three times its size. Wide-eyed and terrified, it sat motionless on the starting pad hearing only the jeering crowds. Eventually the allotted 30 seconds elapsed and the frog was disqualified. Then it jumped – unofficially. The first jump took it 4,2 m (multiply that by three!). The second took it clear into the gasping onlookers whose loyalty to the home side ensured that it never made a third jump, even unofficially. To avoid national humiliation, the Jumping Frog Jubilee rules were changed soon after that, and they now decree that all entrants 'must be at least four (4) inches in length'. Grass Frogs never exceed 2$\frac{1}{2}$ inches. Frog jumping in South Africa became

popular again in the 1970s before television came to the platteland. The doyen of the sport was Piem Fourie of Elsburg. Teams of Cape River Frogs (over 4 inches) were sent to compete in Calaveras on several occasions where they acquitted themselves well. But it was in the small towns of South Africa that the real records were being broken. On 21 May 1977 at the Maroela Spa in Paulpietersburg, athletic history was made when 'Santjie' the Sharp-nosed Grass Frog set the standing world record of 10,3 m.

Piem Fourie wishing his champion Cape River Frog 'Knappie' luck on its departure for the Calaveras County Jumping Frog Jubilee. (The Star, 14 May 1974).

Rivers

Species to look for:

Flat-backed Toad 75   Lemaire's Toad 78   Beira Pygmy Toad 77   Russet-backed Sand Frog 73

Few frogs breed in the large savanna rivers because of the powerful flow and erratic flooding. However, the **Flat-backed Toad** and the **Russet-backed Sand Frog** both call on river sandbanks and manage to find backwaters and pools in which to breed successfully. When the annual floods of the Zambezi recede, the rarely seen **Lemaire's Toad** emerges to breed on the flood-plains. Another flood-plain inhabitant is the **Beira Pygmy Toad**. It is similar in appearance to other species of pygmy toad, but it seldom exceeds 25 mm, and it is listed in the Guinness Book of Records as the smallest toad in the world.

Savanna·river, in which few species of frog generally breed.

Open ground

Species to look for:

Bushveld Rain Frog 68   Whistling Rain Frog 69   Mozambique Rain Frog 69   Bocage's Tree Frog 71

Some frogs are purely terrestrial. On rainy nights the chirping call of the **Bushveld Rain Frogs** can be heard wherever there is suitable soil for them to have made their burrows. Each caller triggers a chain of responding calls from its neighbours. Tunnels are constructed by digging backwards into the soil using a digging tubercle on the heel. Males call from the mouths of their burrows, but as the evening progresses, both males and females emerge and wander about in pursuit of each other. Conventional mounting (amplexus) is impossible with such rotund, short-legged frogs, so they glue themselves together with secretions from the female's back. Physical separation is impossible without tearing the male abdomen. The glued pair lay their eggs in a chamber, about 40 cm below the surface, after which the female secretes the solvent that releases her partner. The pale tadpoles remain in the chamber, feeding off the egg yolk until they metamorphose.

Les Minter

Bushveld Rain Frogs glued together while mating.

GRASSLAND: HIGHVELD INTERIOR AND EASTERN ESCARPMENT

The grasslands of southern Africa are divided by the Drakensberg and Maluti mountain ranges – the highest altitudes in southern Africa. East of these mountains the hills and valleys of the KwaZulu-Natal escarpment receive an annual rainfall of between 800 mm and 1 200 mm. The grass is lush and interspersed with patches of forest. Numerous streams rise in upland marshes and tumble through riverine bush and grassy banks, occasionally spreading into vleis in the broader valleys.

West of the Drakensberg lies the flat highveld plateau, ridged with occasional quartzite outcrops. Frost and fire confine indigenous trees to the protective ridges and river gorges but alien trees have been planted extensively for shade and windbreaks. Rain falls mostly in the summer and the average rainfall decreases towards the west until eventually the grassland blends into semi-desert. Temporary pans are common in the flat areas and streams and vleis feed the major river systems that flow north-east into the Indian Ocean and south-west into the Atlantic. Human activity has modified the grassland considerably. Alien timber trees and fields of maize and other crops have replaced the wild grasses. Pans and vleis have been drained and alien vegetation chokes the banks of streams. Elsewhere over-grazing and excessive burning has stripped vegetation away and allowed waterways to become eroded into dongas with banks of sterile subsoil. These developments have destroyed the natural habitats of many frogs but farms and gardens have created suitable breeding sites and sources of food for a few species.

Pans in grassland are natural breeding sites for numerous species after rain.

Semi-permanent water – streams and farm dams

Species to look for:

Common Platanna 53	Common River Frog 79	Cape River Frog 80
Striped Stream Frog 79	Guttural Toad 75	Karoo Toad 76
Eastern Leopard Toad 75	Raucous Toad 74	Red Toad 77
Yellow-striped Reed Frog 62	Snoring Puddle Frog 89	

One beneficiary of human activity is the **Common Platanna**. They occur in any reasonably permanent water, particularly farm dams. Almost entirely aquatic, they remain submerged just below the surface with forelimbs outstretched to grasp at food. Unlike other southern African frogs, they feed underwater, taking live prey or scavenging detritus. Periodically they surface to gulp air but they also absorb oxygen from the water through the skin.

Platannas have sharp claws on the hind feet which they use to shred food particles. If seized, the frogs rake their captor with their claws while exuding a slippery fluid to help them escape. Sometimes they migrate from one pond to another, digging their claws into the ground to thrust their way clumsily overland.

Calling and mating is done underwater. Inflating a vocal sac like other frogs would upset buoyancy so a buzzing call is made by vibrating cartilage structures in the larynx. Mating pairs indulge in elaborate rolls and loops while depositing eggs on submerged vegetation. Shoals of tadpoles hang in the water at about 45 degrees with their heads down and tails constantly quivering while they extract microscopic particles of food from the water. In past decades Platannas were used for pregnancy testing (if injected with the urine of a pregnant woman, the female Platanna immediately discharges her eggs) and they remain favoured specimens for laboratory dissection.

Common River Frogs are frequently encountered during the day as they sit at the edges of dams or quiet streams and plop into the water as one approaches. They breed in autumn and early winter and the quiet 'kik kik kik kik kerroik' is a familiar sound during both day and night.

Another winter breeder is the **Striped Stream Frog**. Its slender limbs and striking stripes provide remarkably effective camouflage in long grass near water. Its bird-like twittering carries far on crisp winter evenings in the eastern, high-rainfall parts of the grassland. A common toad of the grasslands is the **Guttural Toad**. In spring and summer the gravelly choruses (often mistakenly attributed to bullfrogs) can be heard wherever there is standing water. They happily colonize suburban fish ponds and farm dams, and even electrification suits them, as they often sit under lights gorging themselves on insects. As with all members of the toad family, the eggs are laid in strings of jelly, and a single female lays about 20 000 eggs at a time.

The transparent Platanna tadpole hangs motionless except for a quivering tail-tip.

Grassland

Common River Frog calling from a semi-submerged position at the edge of the dam.

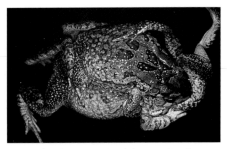

Guttural and Raucous Toads in a mating frenzy in an ornamental pond.

While Guttural Toads breed in standing water, another grassland toad, the **Raucous Toad**, breeds in the quiet reaches of flowing streams. However, human structures such as ornamental fountains sometimes blur the distinction between stationary and flowing water. Under these conditions, Raucous and Guttural Toads frequently hybridize. At the breeding site, calling males become frenzied in anticipation of the arrival of females. Any passing frog is immediately pounced upon by a tangle of frantic males and species recognition seems to fail. Few of the eggs of such mis-matches are viable but those that do survive to adulthood have voices pitched between the high quack of the Raucous Toad and the throaty croak of the Guttural Toad.

Temporary pans and rain pools

Species to look for:

Giant Bullfrog 70	Striped Caco 88	Poynton's Caco 88
Bronze Caco 87	Common Caco 88	Southern Pygmy Toad 77
Amatola Toad 74	Tremolo Sand Frog 72	Natal Sand Frog 73
Painted Reed Frog 64	Striped Grass Frog 83	

Temporary roadside rain pool – breeding site for both the Giant Bullfrog and the tiny Caco.

Summer rains come to the grassland in the form of abrupt, soaking thunderstorms and part of the runoff is contained in temporary rain pools or pans that can vary considerably in size. These make excellent breeding habitats for a number of frog species. Size, pugnaciousness and the extraordinary mating behaviour of the **Giant Bullfrog** set it aside from any other species in southern Africa. Unlike most frogs, males are larger than females and can exceed 200 mm, yet they breed in pools that are only a few centimetres

THE FIRST SOUTH AFRICAN FROGGER

As early as the 16th century explorers were fascinated by the plants and animals of southern Africa, yet little was ever written about the frogs. Only after the arrival of Andrew Smith in 1821 were the frogs of the region formally studied, described and illustrated.

Smith was a Scottish military doctor posted to the frontier town of Grahamstown. He had a great thirst for knowledge and a passion for natural history. In 1825 the Governor of the Cape, Lord Charles Somerset, invited him to establish the South African Museum in Cape Town. For the next thirteen years Smith travelled widely, collecting specimens for his museum and simultaneously acting as diplomat, ethnologist, explorer and spy for the Cape colonial government. He was accompanied on his expeditions by two skilled artists, Charles Bell and George Henry Ford, who meticulously recorded the landscape, the people and the fauna they encountered. Ford's paintings include the earliest known illustrations of South African frogs.

After leaving the Cape in 1838, Smith spent ten years publishing his monumental work, *The Zoology of South Africa*, in a series of illustrated volumes. They included detailed, scientific descriptions of all twenty-six species of South African frogs then known. Fourteen of them had been discovered by Smith himself. A century and a half later zoologists still make use of his original descriptions. Modern froggers will sympathize with the frustrations expressed in Andrew Smith's 1830 account of hunting for the Bubbling Kassina:

"This frog ... is exceedingly noisy during dull weather, or immediately before rain. Many, perhaps twenty persons, were occupied for hours searching for the individuals which first attracted our notice, but no traces of them could be discovered till a Hottentot, noticing a small hole in the ground, suspected what we were in search of was in it. It was the entrance to a burrow, in which was at least one of the individuals which had caused us such anxiety. The secret having been discovered, we procured many specimens."

Dr Andrew Smith

Illustration by George Henry Ford of a Bubbling Kassina in Andrew Smith's, THE ZOOLOGY OF SOUTH AFRICA.

Left: Giant Bullfrog breaking out of its winter cocoon. **Middle:** *Male Bullfrogs fighting at the breeding site.* **Right:** *Male Bullfrog safe-guarding a swarm of tadpoles.*

deep. For most of the year Bullfrogs remain buried more than a metre underground encased in a transparent cocoon that completely covers the entire body, closing all apertures except the nostrils. This extra skin looks like a fitted plastic bag and it reduces moisture loss during the dry winter months. Early summer thunderstorms stimulate the frogs to emerge and for several days following a series of heavy thundershowers they assemble to breed in daylight at shallow, rain-filled depressions and pans.

The choice of shallow water may seem strange for such a large frog but it offers a number of advantages. Temporary pans are free of many of the aquatic predators that feed on eggs and tadpoles in more permanent water. Shallow water also enables the breeding pair to stand on the floor of the pan and raise their hindquarters out of the water as the female produces a small batch of eggs. These are fertilized in the air by the male and then washed away as the pair lower themselves back into the water.

Throughout the short breeding season males emit their deep calf-like bellowing and attack one another viciously with formidable grunting and splashing. The tooth-like projections in the lower jaw, normally used to lock onto their food, are used at the breeding site to fling their opponent away from the female, even while in the process of mating. They often injure and even kill one another in the process.

In the warm, shallow water the eggs hatch quickly. The tadpoles swarm in tight masses that appear to boil as individuals constantly traffic between the aerated surface and food sources on the bottom. A large male attends the tadpole swarm at all times and aggressively snaps at intruders, including humans. Within thirty days of egg-laying, fully metamorphosed frogs are able to leave the water – the quickest development of any highveld species. A singular disadvantage of breeding in shallow water is, of course, the possibility of it drying up. This potential threat is addressed by deliberate parental care. If tadpoles are trapped in a small, drying rain pool, the adult male digs a canal for several metres to a more substantial body of water and the tadpoles swim down the channel to safety.

At the other end of the size scale are the multi-coloured **Cacos** that also breed in temporary rain pools and vleis. They are among the most numerous frogs in southern Africa, yet few people ever see them because of their tiny size, secretive behaviour and colouring. After a highveld thunderstorm almost every inundated patch of grass crackles with the call of the

Common Caco and the sound is often dismissed as that of an insect. But at close quarters the high-pitched explosive 'ticks' are almost painful to the human ear. For a split second the 20 mm caller pumps air with enormous energy into a vocal sac that is almost the size of its body, to create a percussive burst of sound.

Temporary rain pools in barren rocky outcrops are the preferred breeding sites for the **Southern Pygmy Toad**. These small toads occur exclusively in the inland highveld grassland, but several other similar-looking species are found in the bushveld to the north.

Highveld vlei

Southern Pygmy Toad eggs in a shallow rock pool.

Marshes, vleis and seepage

Species to look for:

Natal Leaf-folding Frog 58	Knysna Leaf-folding Frog 58	Mist Belt Chirping Frog 86
Bubbling Kassina 61	Long-toed Tree Frog 59	Rattling Frog 61
Clicking Stream Frog 81		

In the high-rainfall areas of the eastern grassland, small rivulets and marshes develop in the waterlogged ground. Similar habitats are created in vleis where the course of a stream spreads into shallow, marshy ground.

In the course of its evolution the **Long-toed Tree Frog** has moved away from its arboreal past and has adapted to the treeless marshes of the southern Drakensberg foothills. In winter the tussocks of vlei grass are frequently under snow but in summer they are inundated with flood water and provide a breeding ground with limited competition from other species. Little is known about the life of this rare frog, but it is now being presented with a new danger: the marshland to which it has so specifically adapted is flat, well watered and ideal for timber plantations – the greatest threat to this tree frog is trees!

One of the most evocative sounds on a summer evening is the liquid 'quoip' of the **Bubbling Kassina**. This frog is found throughout much of southern Africa in a variety of grassland and savanna habitats. By day the frogs hide in burrows made by other creatures, often some distance from the water. Then, as the late afternoon begins to cool, the ventriloquial calls begin, each one triggering a series of responses from other callers across the veld. As the

sun sets, the calling males walk or run (never hop) down to the water where the chorus becomes intense and competitive. The **Clicking Stream Frog** is found in a variety of damp, cool habitats from the Drakensberg to sea-level, but it appears to favour areas of seepage or moist stream banks to lay its eggs, pressing them into the mud under a thin film of water. From there the emerging tadpoles are able to slip into deeper water to develop. Considerable colour variation can make identification of the adult frogs difficult – individuals from the same breeding population may have totally different patterns and colours – but the diversity is there to confuse the searching instincts of predators.

Dark patterning on the vocal sac helps to conceal the Bubbling Kassina while it calls.

Mountain streams

Species to look for:

Drakensberg River Frog 80   Johnston's River Frog 80   Aquatic River Frog 80
Berg Stream Frog 81   Plain Stream Frog 81

Most River and Stream frogs are found in cool climates and are tolerant of the cold. This is taken to extremes by the large **Aquatic River Frog**. It inhabits cold, clear mountain streams near the summit of the Drakensberg and it survives in temperatures well below freezing. Even the tadpoles have been seen swimming in pools that are covered in ice. A minute shading device in the eye protects it from high-altitude ultra-violet radiation.

The **Berg Stream Frog** and the **Plain Stream Frog** are also high-altitude species and are only found in a restricted section of the Drakensberg mountains, on the grassy banks of mountain streams just below the summit.

Drakensberg gully in the dry season.

PHOTOGRAPHING FROGS

Frog photography can be extremely rewarding and the following guidelines may help to make it so:

• Equipment should be simple and robust enough for fieldwork under difficult conditions. A 35 mm single-lens reflex camera with a 100 mm macro-lens allowing ratios from 1:10 down to 1:1 is ideal. Most video cameras have those capabilities built in.

• Lighting must be sufficient to allow a small aperture for good depth of focus. Direct flash at close quarters over-exposes the foreground, casts black shadows and reflects annoyingly off smooth-skinned frogs. These difficulties can be overcome by using two small flash guns mounted so that their beams diverge slightly. The frog is illuminated by both flashes while the foreground is lit by only one (see diagram). The angle of light also reduces reflections.

• Video cameras operate at low light intensity and the movement of the subject detracts from the shallow field of focus. Prolonged bright lighting would disturb the frog.

• Complete all camera settings before approaching so that the minimum of movement is needed close to the frog.

A simple camera setup for field photography.

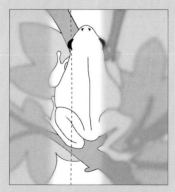

Focusing on the eye brings most visible parts of the frog within the depth of field.

• Ask a companion to hold a torch steady, but not directly on the frog, while you focus.

• Always focus on the eye. Viewers will forgive most imperfections provided the eye is sharp.

• Photograph from a low, frogs-eye-level. Partially over-head shots are seldom pleasing.

• Carry a waterproof covering for equipment. The best frog pictures will often be obtained in the rain.

RECORDING FROG CALLS

Frog calls are very distinctive and good results can be obtained without highly sophisticated equipment. Guidelines that may be useful are:

• A portable recorder with a microphone on an extension lead is the only equipment needed. Manual control of the recording level is preferable as some calls are so short and loud that automatic volume controls cannot function quickly enough.

• Moving very cautiously, place the microphone close to the calling frog without disturbing it. Then move back as far from the frog as the microphone lead allows, set the recording levels for the call and make the recording. Because of the proximity of the microphone, the volume of the call will dominate extraneous sounds.

• A foam-plastic wind shield over the microphone is essential. It reduces wind noise and protects the microphone from moisture and accidental knocks.

FOREST: AFROMONTANE ESCARPMENT, COASTAL BUSH AND RIVERINE FOREST

Southern Africa is not well endowed with natural forest and the little that exists consists of vulnerable patches, constantly threatened by encroaching timber plantations and slash-and-burn farmers in quest of crop-land. But forest is an essential habitat for many frogs.

A forest is defined as an environment where the overhead canopy of trees is closed, giving permanent shade. Such tree growth requires abundant water and suitable conditions arise in three circumstances:

- Afromontane forest occurs on mountain escarpments where moisture-laden air rises, precipitating mist and rain.
- Coastal forest is found on the dunes and hills along the south-east coast of Africa where the climate offers high rainfall and warm humidity during much of the year.
- Riverine forests grow along the banks of rivers and streams, drawing moisture from the watercourse.

All three forest types support a wide diversity of inter-dependent plant and animal species. This is a particularly benign environment for frogs. The forest canopy regulates temperature extremes, keeping the interior shady and cool in summer and protecting it from wind and frost in winter. The constant cover restricts evaporation and maintains a permanently damp, humid environment where frogs can thrive without threat of desiccation. One-fifth of the frog species of southern Africa are permanent forest dwellers, despite the fact that only one two-hundredth of the surface area of the region is under natural forest.

Afromontane forest in KwaZulu-Natal.

Cultivated plantations of imported timber trees such as pine or eucalypts now cover much of the high-rainfall areas of southern Africa but they support little biodiversity and do not offer the ecological benefits of natural forests.

Mountain streams

Species to look for:

Natal Ghost Frog 56	Southern Ghost Frog 55	Table Mountain Ghost Frog 55
Kloof Frog 65	Clicking Stream Frog 81	

Mountain stream.

Above: *Tracks left by Ghost Frog tadpoles on rocks in the stream.* **Right**: *Ghost Frog tadpole*

Afromontane forest is invariably found on steep slopes with high rainfall where mountain torrents plunge over rapids and waterfalls. Very few of the common tadpole predators like fish, turtles, dragonfly larvae or even bacteria can tolerate these fast-flowing streams. Indeed, most species of tadpole would be unable to survive in the rushing water. But those of the **Ghost Frog** have adapted to take advantage of mountain streams.

The tadpoles have enormous mouths spanning the width of the body and they are equipped with sixteen rows of teeth. They move about the stream bed by pulling themselves over the rocks by their teeth while simultaneously eating off the algae. They even climb waterfalls in this manner. The random wandering of the tadpoles can be seen as narrow tracks of cleaned rock surface under the clear water.

During the breeding season the frogs develop sharp asperities on their fingers, arms and under the jaw, and they use these to caress each other prior to mating. Eggs are laid in hidden recesses next to running water. Metamorphosis is slow in the cool mountain water and the tadpole stage lasts more than a year. Breeding takes place before the onset of rains because streams that are flowing in the dry season are most likely to be perennial, so tadpoles are assured of not being stranded in a drying watercourse the following season.

Forest

Ghost Frogs are extremely secretive. They have wide, T-shaped adhesive pads on their fingers which enable them to climb slippery surfaces, and favourite retreats are the dark recesses behind waterfalls. Although seldom seen, the clear whistling notes of their calls can sometimes be heard above the noise of rushing streams.

Adaptation to breeding in fast-flowing water has trapped some species of Ghost Frog within the limits of their specific catchment area of mountain streams. The **Table Mountain Ghost Frog** for instance, is found only on Table Mountain, unable to cross the lower valleys that lack its specialized habitat.

Eggs of the Kloof Frog with an almost hatched tadpole slipping from the softened egg mass into the water below.

In the darkest parts of the forests of KwaZulu-Natal where the seepage trickles into streams with inaccessible, slippery banks, one finds the **Kloof Frog**. They can be distinguished from Ghost Frogs by their horizontal pupils. They are sharp-nosed, athletic jumpers with wide, spatula-like adhesive pads on their toes. They are capable of climbing vertical, wet, slippery surfaces and there, safe from the most intrepid predator, they lay their eggs in a clear jelly mass on vegetation and rocks overhanging the water. Initially the egg mass is quite firm but, as the tadpoles develop, it softens and the newly hatched tadpoles slip gently into the water below.

Forest floor

Species to look for:

Transvaal Forest Rain Frog 68	Plaintive Rain Frog 68	Plain Rain Frog 67
Strawberry Rain Frog 67	Highland Rain Frog 69	Spotted Rain Frog 68
Shovel-footed Squeaker 71	Bush Squeaker 78	Northern Squeaker 78
Cave Squeaker 78		

Plaintive Rain Frog calling on the forest floor amidst layers of fallen leaves and humus.

The entire life cycle of **Rain Frogs** is completed in the deep layers of fallen leaves and humus on the forest floor. There are fourteen species of Rain Frogs, seven of which are forest dwellers. They all have dumpy bodies from which the head barely protrudes and, together with the extremely short legs, this adds to their corpulent appearance. They feed on woodlice and other small, slow-moving creatures that breed in the leaf litter and their mouths are set in a flattened face with forward-looking eyes suitable for close-up, bi-focal vision of the passing fare. The carpet of fallen leaves

Les Minter

Rain Frog eggs. Extra egg-less jelly capsules provide fluid for the tadpoles.

offers a retreat in which the slow-moving Rain Frogs can burrow to escape predators but, if confronted, they inflate themselves until they are almost spherical in order to appear larger than they really are. The distended body deters would-be predators such as snakes, but it evidently fails to deter bushpigs that eat Rain Frogs like truffles if they find them.

Rain Frogs lay their eggs in underground chambers, using hard, horny tubercles on the hind feet to burrow into the forest floor and excavate their nests. These are often sited under rocks or logs for greater protection. The unique manner in which male and female Rain Frogs are glued together while mating is described and illustrated on page 23. The eggs have large whitish yolks covered in a thick viscous jelly. Several egg-less jelly capsules are also laid in the clutch. As the tadpoles develop the jelly softens into a fluid in which they wriggle about, the empty capsules providing extra fluid. The pale-coloured tadpoles absorb the egg yolk as they grow and require no other sustenance until they are fully metamorphosed frogs.

In the forests of KwaZulu-Natal the **Bush Squeaker** is seldom seen, yet their persistent, squeaky calls are triggered by the slightest fall of rain or mist and can be heard from almost every clump of bush. Easily mistaken for the sound of an insect, the call seems to cut through all other noise and becomes part of one's subconscious awareness of the wet weather. The tiny, illusive frogs are cryptically coloured to match the loose leaves under which they hide.

Like Rain Frogs, Bush Squeakers breed on the forest floor and have dispensed with an aquatic tadpole. Eggs are scattered among the leaf litter and metamorphosis proceeds right through to the stage that a perfect, 3 mm miniature frog emerges from the egg.

Seepage and the splash of waterfalls

Species to look for:

Bainskloof Chirping Frog 85	Cape Chirping Frog 85	Drews's Chirping Frog 85
Natal Chirping Frog 85	Villiers's Chirping Frog 85	Hogsback Frog 86

Because forests exist only where water is plentiful, sloping ground frequently oozes with excess moisture so that moss accumulates and rock surfaces become slippery with algae. Similar conditions occur where the splash of waterfalls keeps the ground permanently saturated. Tiny **Chirping Frogs,** in a bewildering array of different colour forms, inhabit these damp places, both in the forest and in adjacent fynbos and grassland. They lay small clutches of eggs in wet depressions concealed by overhanging rocks or plants. While the frogs are seldom more than 20 mm, the eggs are relatively enormous – 4 mm in diameter with a jelly capsule that swells to 8 mm. Tadpoles develop after about ten days. They are colourless except for dark tails that help conceal them as they squirm about in the damp moss until they have metamorphosed into fully formed miniature frogs.

Hogsback Frog nest in a cavity below the leaf-litter.

Chirping Frog among the moss.

The ability to breed without having to return to open water offers considerable advantages. It reduces the risks of predation, desiccation, disease and the washing away of eggs and tadpoles. It probably evolved at a time when the African continent had a wetter climate than now and when much of the southern part of the continent was covered in rain forest. As the climate became drier, the forests retreated, leaving only isolated

Forest waterfall in the Hogsback mountains.

islands in an expanding sea of grassland and savanna. Frog populations that had adapted to damp conditions became marooned in the remnant patches where they continued to evolve independently into different species.

The different species of Chirping Frogs are examples. Six species have been identified in southern Africa, each one with a very localized distribution. Four are found in the Western Cape and two in KwaZulu-Natal. The Western Cape species are identical in appearance and can be identified only by small differences in their call and through DNA analysis in a laboratory.

The **Hogsback Frog** has also developed a way of life specifically suited to the seepage banks and waterfalls and this specialization confines it to the Amatola forests around the village of Hogsback in the Eastern Cape. Along the forest paths that lead from one waterfall to another, the piping notes of male Hogsback Frogs can be heard clearly above the rush of falling water. The callers are only about 20 mm long and coloured in the brown and coppery shades of decaying leaves. Unlike Rain Frogs, the males tunnel head first into the forest floor. They have hard, chisel-like snouts with which they excavate spherical burrows

Forest Tree Frogs wrestling for dominance of the call site.

about the size of a golf ball. Females are attracted by the calling males and the mating couples enter the burrows to lay about 15 or 20 eggs. The entire metamorphosis takes place within the nest and after three or four weeks the minute frogs emerge from their underground nursery to mature in the forest leaf litter.

Trees

Species to look for:

Forest Tree Frog 59   Spotted Tree Frog 59   Silver Tree Frog 59
Chirinda Toad 78

Relatively few species of Tree Frog inhabit the forests of southern Africa; most southern African Tree Frogs occur in savanna woodland. The sharp quack of the **Forest Tree Frog** mating call is made from a carefully selected position in a tree close to water. Males defend their call site from other males by emitting a buzzing territorial call and, if necessary, wrestling with the intruder to drive him away. Once a female has been attracted, the pair descend to the ground to lay eggs in a sheltered position on a stream bank. As soon as the tadpoles begin to hatch, they squirm in a convulsive mass towards the water. There the long, eel-like tadpoles complete their metamorphosis. The urge for the emerging tadpoles to get to the water is powerful, and the squirming mass is capable of wriggling its way over almost any obstacle to reach its goal. Finding food in trees is quite demanding and these appealing bright green Tree Frogs with their large night-vision eyes and long adhesive toes, leap agilely about in pursuit of moths and other flying insects.

Perhaps the most unusual use of forest trees is made by the rare **Chirinda Toad** from eastern Zimbabwe and neighbouring Mozambique. It lays its eggs in pools of water trapped by the buttress roots of forest trees. The fluted milkwood tree, *Chrysophyllum gorungosum*, grows only in this area, and is favoured by these small toads.

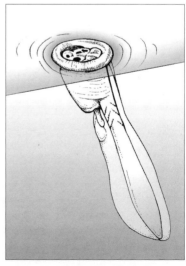

The tadpoles are specially adapted to this unusual breeding site. The head bears a crown of spongy tissue surrounding the eyes and nostrils. While the tadpole feeds on the living walls of the pool, the crown rests at the surface and absorbs oxygen from the air through a network of blood vessels in the spongy tissue. The gills of a normal tadpole would be useless for respiration in the stagnant, de-oxygenated water, but that water is also unsuitable for most tadpole predators. Relative freedom from predation means that the female need only lay about a hundred eggs at a time, giving the frog a considerable advantage.

Chirinda Toad tadpole (illustration after A Channing).

EVOLUTION OF SOUTHERN AFRICAN FROGS

Period	million years ago	Evolutionary landmarks
Quaternary	0–1	Numerous large birds and mammals become extinct. Frog populations decline. (6th Extinction)
Tertiary	25	Early Platanna fossil, **Xenopus stromeri**, from Namibia. Modern mammals, reptiles and amphibians develop.
Cretaceous	65	Dinosaurs become extinct. (5th Extinction)
	120	Earliest southern African fossil of a jumping frog resembling Platanna, **Xenopoides.**
Jurassic	120-200	Reptiles prolific throughout southern Africa.
Triassic	200	Mammal-like reptiles become extinct. (4th Extinction)
	230	Earliest tail-less amphibian fossil (Madagascar), **Triadobatrachus**, probable ancestor of modern frogs.
Permian	250	Massive extinctions of species through seismic activity and the break-up of Gondwana. (3rd Extinction)
	280	Earliest southern African amphibian fossil, **Rhinesuchus.**
Carboniferous	350	Large numbers of amphibian orders develop, some several metres in length. Amphibians become the most prolific vertebrates until the late Permian. Early reptiles develop from amphibian ancestors.
Devonian	360	Earliest known amphibian fossil, **Ichthyostega**. 70 cm long with limbs that enabled it to walk on land, possibly to migrate from one body of water to another.
	370	Multiple asteroid impact causes extinction of majority of marine and plant species. (2nd Extinction)
	400	Freshwater lobe-fin fishes (**Rhipidistia**) develop short, robust fins for walking on the lake-floor, as well as lungs that enable them to survive drought.

Modern frog

Xenopoides

Triadobatrachus

Rhinesuchus

Ichthyostega

Rhipidistian fish

FYNBOS: SOUTHERN AND WESTERN CAPE COASTAL REGION

Fynbos, the predominant vegetation in the Cape Floral Kingdom, is renowned for the beauty and diversity of its proteas, ericas and other plants. Although the term 'fynbos' is botanical, it is used here to denote the geographical region that lies between the Karoo and the southern and western sea shores. The area is comparatively small – about 90 000 square kilometres or 3% of southern Africa as a whole – yet it has 46% of the plant species of the region and 28% of the frogs.

Even more impressive than merely the number of species in the area is the high proportion of endemics, i.e. species that occur in this area and nowhere else. It is almost as if the fynbos were an oceanic island, separated from the rest of Africa.

Topographically the fynbos region extends from coastal dunes to mountain ranges. On the seaward escarpments precipitation often exceeds 1 000 mm per year, while the rain-shadows in the lee of the mountains receive less than half of that. Along its northern edge the fynbos is arid and merges with the semi-desert of the hinterland. In contrast with the rest of southern Africa, the fynbos region receives most of its rainfall during winter. This wide range of climatic conditions and habitats give the region its unique diversity of frog life.

Within the fynbos region there are pockets of forests and the frogs that occur in them are discussed in the previous chapter. The frogs of these forests are largely endemic so that altogether almost one fifth of all southern African frogs occur in this small region and nowhere else.

Fynbos, forest and mountains in the Western Cape.

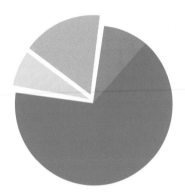

- Fynbos endemics
  (16 species)

- Forest frogs endemic to the Fynbos Geographic Region
  (18 species)

- Non-endemic species in the Fynbos Geographic Region
  (12 species)

- All other southern African species
  (92 species)

FYNBOS ENDEMICS

Cape Mountain Rain Frog	*Breviceps montanus*
Cape Rain Frog	*Breviceps gibbosus*
Sand Rain Frog	*Breviceps rosei*
Western Leopard Toad	*Bufo pantherinus*
Sand Toad	*Bufo angusticeps*
Cape Caco	*Cacosternum capense*
Tradouw Mountain Toad	*Capensibufo tradouwi*
Rose's Mountain Toad	*Capensibufo rosei*
Hewitt's Ghost Frog	*Heleophryne hewitti*
Cape Ghost Frog	*Heleophryne purcelli*
Arum Lily Reed Frog	*Hyperolius horstocki*
Micro Frog	*Microbatrachella capensis*
Marsh Frog	*Poyntonia paludicola*
Banded Stream Frog	*Strongylopus bonaspei*
Cape Sand Frog	*Tomopterna delalandii*
Cape Platanna	*Xenopus gilli*

FOREST FROGS ENDEMIC TO THE FYNBOS GEOGRAPHIC REGION

Bainskloof Chirping Frog	*Arthroleptella bicolor*
Cape Chirping Frog	*Arthroleptella lightfooti*
Drews's Chirping Frog	*Arthroleptella drewsii*
Villiers's Chirping Frog	*Arthroleptella villiersi*
Strawberry Rain Frog	*Breviceps acutirostris*
Plain Rain Frog	*Breviceps fuscus*
Southern Ghost Frog	*Heleophryne regis*
Table Mountain Ghost Frog	*Heleophryne rosei*

NON-ENDEMIC SPECIES IN THE FYNBOS GEOGRAPHIC REGION

Karoo Toad	*Bufo gariepensis*	Cape River Frog	*Afrana Fuscigula*
Eastern Leopard Toad	*Bufo pardalis*	Striped Stream Frog	*Strongylopus fasciatus*
Raucous Toad	*Bufo rangeri*	Clicking Stream Frog	*Strongylopus grayii*
Knysna Leaf-foldingFrog	*Afrixalus knysnae*	Tandy'd Sand Frog	*Tomopterna tandyi*
Rattling Frog	*Semnodactylus weallii*	Common Caco	*Cacosternum boettgeri*
Common Platanna	*Xenopus laevis*	Bronze Caco	*Cacosternum nanum*

Frogs and Frogging in Southern Africa

Western Leopard Toad showing the distinctive pink parotid glands.

An Arum Lily Reed Frog taking up a position in a lily.

Permanent, semi-permanent pans; vleis and farm dams

Species to look for:

Arum Lily Reed Frog 62	Western Leopard Toad 75	Raucous Toad 74
Cape Platanna 53	Common Platanna 53	Cape River Frog 80
Striped Stream Frog 79		

Look into the flower of an arum lily growing at the edge of a fynbos pan and there is every chance of finding an **Arum Lily Reed Frog**. Its cream colouring blends well with the lily and a dusting of pollen usually improves the camouflage. The endearing posture is actually a lethal ambush for insects visiting the flower. By night the frogs become darker and they move to reed stems or lily leaves to call and to mate. Eggs are laid underwater among the roots of aquatic plants.

Like other Reed Frogs, the Arum Lily Reed Frog displays the vivid pink or orange inner surfaces of the limbs as it leaps from potential danger. They are the largest of the southern African Reed Frogs, being 5 mm or 10 mm longer than any other species.

The fynbos is also home to the largest southern African toad, the **Western Leopard Toad**. For many years it and the **Eastern Leopard Toad** were considered the same species although they are widely separated geographically. Recent work by John Poynton and Angelo Lambiris has now clarified the status of the Western Leopard Toad as a fynbos endemic. Despite its size it is not often seen because it emerges only briefly to breed for a few days in August, which accounts for its local name of 'August Toad'.

Two species of platanna are found in fynbos – the widely distributed **Common Platanna** and the endemic **Cape Platanna**. Both species are highly aquatic, seldom emerging from the water. The latter is rare and in danger of extinction because of the destruction of its habitat. The Cape Platanna appears to be successful only in natural wetlands in the Cape Peninsula and the adjacent sandy flats. When these dry out in the summer months, the frogs bury themselves in the damp mud and re-emerge when the ponds refill with autumn rain. Recently, however, the drying of Cape wetlands has often been permanent – the result of drainage for urbanization

Les Minter

More extensive webbing distinguishes the Cape River Frog (right) *from the Common River Frog.*

Temporary pan in the fynbos – possible Micro Frog habitat.

or agriculture rather than natural seasonal change – and there has been no autumn reprieve for the buried platannas. Common Platannas, on the other hand, migrate more readily overland when their habitats are destroyed and they successfully occupy a wide range of water bodies including man-made dams and ditches. There is also a tendency for the two species to hybridize and in these circumstances the genes of the larger and more aggressive Common Platanna dominate.

It is probable that frogs that were once endemic to the Western Cape have spread outwards, colonizing other parts of southern Africa. The **Cape River Frog** may be an example. It is a large frog that breeds in deep permanent water and is particularly common in farm dams. The proliferation of dams may have assisted it to extend its distribution well into grassland and savanna regions where it now competes with the very similar looking Common River Frog.

Temporary pans and vleis

Species to look for:

Micro Frog 88	Bronze Caco 87	Common Caco 88
Cape Caco 87	Sand Toad 74	Karoo Toad 76
Cape Sand Frog 72	Knysna Leaf-folding Frog 58	

The 16 mm **Micro Frog** is the smallest species in Africa and is in danger of extinction. It occurs in a variety of colours and is similar in appearance to the widespread **Common Caco** and **Bronze Caco**. Once common on the sandy flats between Cape Town and Stellenbosch, its habitat has been greatly reduced by housing and other developments and it has not been recorded in that area for several decades. Breeding is now confined to temporary pans in the fynbos between Hangklip and Hermanus. Compounding its demise is the fact that the tadpoles of the Micro Frog take from June until December to metamorphose and in that time their breeding pans sometimes dry up.

The **Sand Toad** breeds in much the same habitat in the sandy flats, but its tadpoles metamorphose and leave the water before the end of the winter rainy season. They are thus exposed to less natural danger than the Micro Frog but are still showing some signs of decline because of the destruction of breeding sites.

Open fynbos

Species to look for:

Sand Rain Frog 67   Cape Rain Frog 66   Cape Mountain Rain Frog 66

Cape Rain Frog

In addition to the Rain Frogs found in the Western Cape forests, three species are found in the open fynbos. The **Cape Rain Frog** is the most commonly seen because it favours suburban gardens. It is the largest of all Rain Frogs, sometimes reaching 60 mm in length and, like all Rain Frogs, it breeds and spends much of its time in underground tunnels. The **Sand Rain Frog** and **Cape Mountain Rain Frog** are smaller and seldom seen as they are confined to the sandveld and rocky mountain slopes.

Mountain streams and seepage

Species to look for:

Cape Ghost Frog 55	Hewitt's Ghost Frog 55	Tradouw Mountain Toad 76
Rose's Mountain Toad 76	Banded Stream Frog 79	Clicking Stream Frog 81
Marsh Frog 88	Cape Chirping Frog 85	Bainskloof Chirping Frog 85
Drews's Chirping Frog 85	Villiers's Chirping Frog 85	

One of the most unusual endemic toads of the fynbos region is the diminutive **Rose's Mountain Toad**. It breeds in shallow pools and sponges high in the mountains of the Cape Peninsula, laying strings of eggs in which the jelly is constricted between each egg, giving the appearance of a string of beads. This toad has no tympanum and no call has ever been heard, even during the peak of the breeding season. Curiously, the very similar-looking **Tradouw Mountain Toad** from the nearby mountains in the Tulbach-Worcester area, does call and does have a tympa-

Pools of seeping water at the source of a mountain stream.

num. Its voice is a discordant, creaking sound. Three species of Stream Frog are found in the fynbos region and, although superficially similar, they are not difficult to distinguish from one another. The endemic species – the **Banded Stream Frog** – is found in marshy areas and seepage zones on mountain slopes. It only occurs in completely natural, undisturbed fynbos, unlike the more widespread **Striped Stream Frog** and **Clicking Stream Frog** that both breed in permanent or temporary man-made environments. The eggs of the Banded Stream Frog are laid on moist ground close to the water's edge and the tadpoles slip into the water as they hatch.

Marshes and seepage zones on high mountain slopes are also home to the recently discovered **Marsh Frog**. For some time, hikers in the mountains above Stellenbosch had been bringing a strange little frog with white stripes on its face to the Jonkershoek Conservation Station for identification. Quite independently of one another, two zoologists, Richard Boycott and Alan Channing, each began compiling the scientific description of what was clearly a new species. Fortunately they learnt of each other's work and combined their efforts, thus avoiding confusion. So different and fragmented are the various components of the fynbos biome that even today, after centuries of biological investigation, new species – and in this instance, a new genus – can still be discovered.

One of the colour variations of the Banded Stream Frog.

THE SIXTH EXTINCTION –
ARE FROGS DYING TO TELL US SOMETHING?

Frog populations throughout the world have crashed dramatically in the last twenty years. Deforestation, wetland draining and pollution are immediately obvious causes. But other, more fundamental, man-made impacts are causing population declines in 'pristine' habitats such as national parks and remote rain-forests. Reductions in atmospheric ozone levels are allowing increased UV-radiation, pollutants are accumulating in natural systems and bacterial and virus distribution is accelerating across the globe. Because of their dual aquatic and terrestrial life, their porous skins and exposed eggs, frogs are particularly vulnerable to environmental disturbances. What is killing them now could, if allowed to proceed, eventually destroy more resilient forms of life such as human beings.

Palaeontologists recognize six periods in the history of the earth when catastrophic events caused vast numbers of species to become extinct. The sixth of these mass extinctions is currently in progress. It is caused by the explosion of human population throughout the planet and the consequent environmental impact.

Extinction	Period	Million years ago	Cause	Main victims
1st	Late Ordovician	420	Global cooling	Marine invertebrates and plants
2nd	Late Devonian	360	Multiple asteroid impact	Marine invertebrates and plants
3rd	End Permian	250	Seismic and volcanic activity continental drift and CO_2 poisoning	Four fifths of all plant and animal life
4th	Late Triassic	215	Double asteroid impact	Mammal-like reptiles and gymnosperm plants
5th	End Cretaceous	60	Single asteroid impact	Dinosaurs
6th	End Quaternary	1	Human overpopulation and consumption of resources	Mammals, birds and amphibians

After J.M. Anderson (ed), Towards Gondwana Alive

DESERT AND SEMI-DESERT: THE ARID WEST

A quarter of southern Africa (much of Namibia, Northern Cape, parts of Botswana and the Karoo) receives less than 200 mm average rainfall a year. The low precipitation is erratic and several years may see no rain. This is a hostile environment to any form of life and for frogs it is particularly threatening. At each stage of their lives – the shell-less egg, the aquatic tadpole and the permeable-skinned adult – they are vulnerable to desiccation, yet several species tolerate the arid climate and at least seven are found nowhere else.

The number and variety of frogs that venture into desert areas fluctuate with the erratic rainfall and this chapter deals with those species that regularly inhabit and successfully breed in arid conditions.

Sand dunes

Species to look for:

Desert Rain Frog 68

South of the Gariep River around Port Nolloth the desert dunes are sparsely covered by succulent scrubs. Loose sand is constantly driven by strong winds, precipitation is minimal and mostly in the form of cold sea mists. There is no natural surface water at all. This is the habitat of the **Desert Rain Frog**, which has a number of unique adaptations to its harsh surroundings. The hands and feet have a thick, fleshy webbing to act as paddles in the loose sand. This

Namib desert dunes and dry watercourse.

Desert Rain Frog using its paddle-like feet on sand.

Vascular skin on the underside of the Desert Rain Frog.

frog hunts insects at night and its distinctive tracks are visible on dunes in the early morning before the wind erases them.

By day the sand is dry at the surface, but below about 10 cm it retains some moisture from the evening fog and the frog spends the daylight hours at this level. The skin on the belly is paper-thin with an extensive network of veins near the surface, and it is presumed that where it rests on the damp sand underground, it absorbs moisture through this vascular membrane. So thin is this skin that it easily bursts when the frog is lifted without support under the belly. In defence against such a mishap, the frogs emit a squeaky wail and secrete a distasteful, milky fluid if molested.

Regrettably, the restricted habitat of the Desert Rain Frog is being strip-mined for diamonds, so that this rare and highly specialized frog is now faced with imminent extinction.

Rocky outcrops

Species to look for:

Namaqua Rain Frog 67   Southern Pygmy Toad 77   Marbled Rubber Frog 54

Weathering of the desert landscape leaves isolated granite outcrops with stratified rock shelves. Deep recesses in these rocky hills hold small amounts of moisture and are cool enough to prevent a frog from desiccating in the midday sun. If rain has fallen, they may ooze a trickle of water into a rocky pool.

Such parsimonious resources are adequate for **Marbled Rubber Frogs**. They have flattened bodies with limbs projecting sideways to enable them to slither between narrow cracks in the rock where they remain throughout the heat of the day. After rain, calling males congregate at the edges of pools where rainwater has collected to depths of a few centimetres. If one male comes too close to another the latter defends his call site by wrestling with the intruder in the water. Both call aggressively throughout the tussle until one, usually the intruder, retires from the scene. Females are attracted to the call site to mate and about 100 eggs are laid at the bottom of the pool. The tadpoles hatch within three or four days. They are severely preyed upon by dragonfly larvae and only a small proportion survive.

Rainwater pool in a rocky desert outcrop.

Sharing the rock pools is a subspecies of the **Southern Pygmy Toad**. They can breed in even shallower pools of water than the Marbled Rubber Frog and have adapted further to desert conditions by retreating deep into mud crevices in dried up pans. From here they emerge in their hundreds to breed when the rare rains refill the pan. As the shallow water warms up in the sun it accelerates metamorphosis so that the vulnerable tadpole stage is kept as short as possible. The shallow water also harbours fewer dragonfly larvae and other predators than deeper, more permanent pools.

River beds

Species to look for:

Tremolo Sand Frog 72	Cape River Frog 80	Van Dijk's River Frog 80
Common Platanna 53	Paradise Toad 77	Western Olive Toad 76

Not every frog in the desert is adapted exclusively to that environment. The **Tremolo Sand Frog** is predominantly a savanna and grassland species but it survives in river beds that rise in the wetter hinterland and dissipate into the sands of the Namib desert. These erratic watercourses are dry for most of the time but occasional heavy rains inland bring them down in spate, bearing with them populations of Sand Frogs and other species, such as the **Cape River Frog** and even the highly aquatic **Common Platanna**. As the floodwaters settle, the frogs breed in remnant pools. Sand Frogs bury themselves in the river sand during the day, River Frogs take shelter in crevices and Platannas remain in the pools, burrowing into the mud if the water dries up. It is uncertain whether these populations are self-sustaining or whether they all eventually perish and are replenished by subsequent floods.

The Kuiseb River – one of several that bring frogs down into the Namib during floods.

In the fascinating, austere landscape of the Richtersveld National Park a new species – the **Paradise Toad** – was recently discovered by the Park Warden, Harold Braack. It breeds in the rare springs and pools that form in remote, arid kloofs. Heavy rains are evidently so unusual in the area that, when they do occur, strings of eggs and tadpoles are swept away by the unexpected torrents.

Left: *The strange Richtersveld landscape – home of the Paradise Toad.* **Right:** *Namaqualand rain pool.*

Rain pools and pans

Species to look for:

Namaqua Caco 87   Namaqua Stream Frog 81   Spotted Rubber Frog 54
Karoo Toad 76

In the rocky hills of the Namaqualand escarpment the **Namaqua Stream Frog** lays its eggs in moist embankments around temporary pools. It is very similar to the Clicking Stream Frog of the higher rainfall areas, but the call is a low, melodious trill as opposed to the sharp, percussive sound of the Clicking Stream Frog.

The transformation of Namaqualand into a floral wonderland in spring is well known. At the same time pools of spring rainwater collect in depressions that are almost invisible during the dry season. Once filled with muddy water, they are soon fringed with short grass and flowers. An abundance of bird life and frogs gather there, including the small, pale-coloured **Namaqua Cacos**. They seem to appear quite miraculously at these small oases and their ability to endure the long intervening dry season is not well understood. They breed rapidly and when they metamorphose, the young frogs are almost as large as the adults.

PHROG PHILATELY

In July 2000 the South African Post Office issued a series of stamps depicting some of the colourful frogs of the country. The designs by Chris van Rooyen were based on photographs that appear in this book.

Desert and semi-desert

KEY TO THE MAIN IDENTIFICATION GROUPS

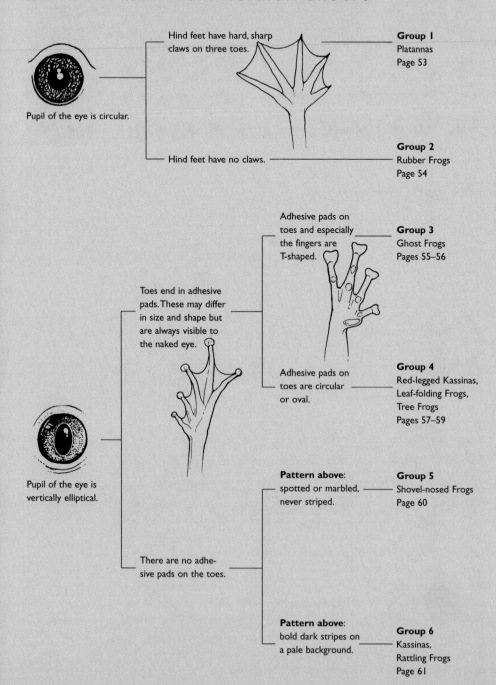

Pupil of the eye is circular.

Hind feet have hard, sharp claws on three toes.

Group 1
Platannas
Page 53

Hind feet have no claws.

Group 2
Rubber Frogs
Page 54

Toes end in adhesive pads. These may differ in size and shape but are always visible to the naked eye.

Adhesive pads on toes and especially the fingers are T-shaped.

Group 3
Ghost Frogs
Pages 55–56

Adhesive pads on toes are circular or oval.

Group 4
Red-legged Kassinas,
Leaf-folding Frogs,
Tree Frogs
Pages 57–59

Pupil of the eye is vertically elliptical.

There are no adhesive pads on the toes.

Pattern above: spotted or marbled, never striped.

Group 5
Shovel-nosed Frogs
Page 60

Pattern above: bold dark stripes on a pale background.

Group 6
Kassinas,
Rattling Frogs
Page 61

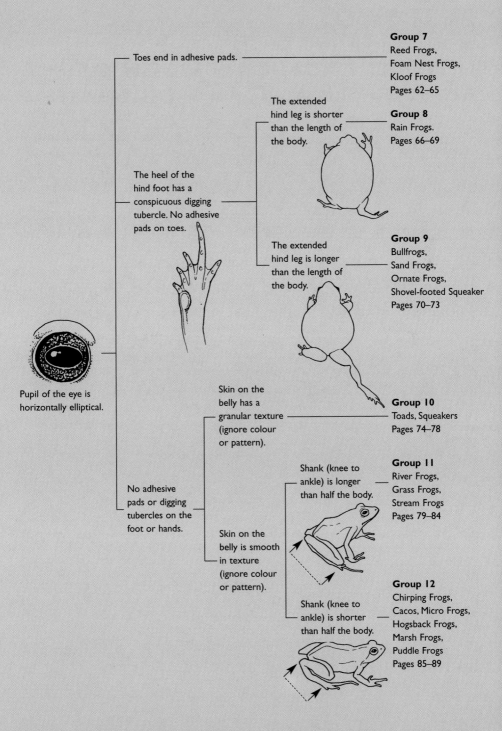

Pupil of the eye is horizontally elliptical.

Toes end in adhesive pads.

Group 7
Reed Frogs,
Foam Nest Frogs,
Kloof Frogs
Pages 62–65

The heel of the hind foot has a conspicuous digging tubercle. No adhesive pads on toes.

The extended hind leg is shorter than the length of the body.

Group 8
Rain Frogs.
Pages 66–69

The extended hind leg is longer than the length of the body.

Group 9
Bullfrogs,
Sand Frogs,
Ornate Frogs,
Shovel-footed Squeaker
Pages 70–73

Skin on the belly has a granular texture (ignore colour or pattern).

Group 10
Toads, Squeakers
Pages 74–78

No adhesive pads or digging tubercles on the foot or hands.

Shank (knee to ankle) is longer than half the body.

Group 11
River Frogs,
Grass Frogs,
Stream Frogs
Pages 79–84

Skin on the belly is smooth in texture (ignore colour or pattern).

Shank (knee to ankle) is shorter than half the body.

Group 12
Chirping Frogs,
Cacos, Micro Frogs,
Hogsback Frogs,
Marsh Frogs,
Puddle Frogs
Pages 85–89

PART TWO

FIELD IDENTIFICATION: DESCRIPTIONS OF ALL SOUTHERN AFRICAN FROG SPECIES

Much of the enjoyment of observing frogs in the wild comes from knowing what species is being observed. This chapter divides all southern African species into twelve groups. To identify a frog, first work out which group it belongs to by selecting from the choice of features given in the key. Once its group has been determined, compare it with the descriptions and illustrations in that group to arrive at a positive identification.

A useful technique is to place the specimen temporarily in a clear plastic bag. Inflate the bag so that the frog can be seen clearly through the taut walls. Once it has been identified, always release the frog in the same place it was found.

GIVE PARTICULAR ATTENTION TO THE FOLLOWING:	
Locality	The place where a frog is found is a useful clue to its identity. It is unlikely that a species will be found very far from the range indicated on the map (although it can very occasionally happen). Descriptions of similar-looking species in each group are arranged geographically from south to north to facilitate comparisons.
Size	The measurements given indicate the size of an average adult from the tip of the snout to the end of the rump (i.e. excluding the legs). There will be some variation around this average.
Description	The features that most clearly distinguish one species from other similar species are shown in bold type. Compare the specimen with the photograph, remembering that sometimes frogs of the same species vary considerably in colour and pattern. The text indicates the extent to which colour variability can be expected.
	Where several species are very similar (e.g. the Dwarf Leaf-folding Frogs), a general description is given, followed by individual descriptions emphasizing the points of difference between each species. This allows easy direct comparisons.
Habitat	Physical surroundings, vegetation, veld type, amount of cover, the call site and the way the specimen behaves in the habitat are often useful clues.
Call	The frog's call, if heard, is a very reliable way of identifying the species. Calls are difficult to verbalize and it is recommended that you make tape recordings in the field and refer to the compact disc enclosed with this book. Calls recorded are marked CD in the text.

GROUP 1

PLATANNAS

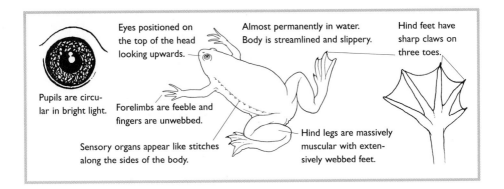

Eyes positioned on the top of the head looking upwards.

Almost permanently in water. Body is streamlined and slippery.

Hind feet have sharp claws on three toes.

Pupils are circular in bright light.

Forelimbs are feeble and fingers are unwebbed.

Sensory organs appear like stitches along the sides of the body.

Hind legs are massively muscular with extensively webbed feet.

Cape Platanna *Xenopus gilli*
40–60 mm. *Above:* Pale grey with two irregular, broad, **dark stripes down the back**. No tentacle below the eye. *Below:* **Yellow with black spots and vermiculations**. *Limbs:* Grey webbing. *Habitat:* Natural pools in fynbos. *Call:* Metallic underwater buzzes, about two per second.

Cape Platanna

Tropical Platanna *Xenopus muelleri*
50–90 mm. *Above:* Mottled, not striped. **A tentacle, about as long as the diameter of the eye, protrudes under the eye.** *Below:* Grey and orange. *Limbs:* **Inner legs and webbing orange.** *Habitat:* Savanna pans with semi-permanent standing water. *Call:* Sharp percussive rapping, about eight per second, underwater.

Tropical Platanna

Common Platanna *Xenopus laevis*
60–100 mm. *Above:* Dark grey-brown, sometimes mottled or stippled. **No tentacle (or just a minute one) below the eye.** *Below:* Off-white, sometimes with grey spots or tinged with yellow. *Limbs:* Webbing grey or slightly yellow but **not orange**. *Habitat:* Any reasonably permanent body of water. *Call:* A constant, undulating buzzing, underwater. CD

● Cape Platanna
● Tropical Platanna

Common Platanna ●

Common Platanna

Platannas

GROUP 2

RUBBER FROGS

Skin is smooth and rubbery.

Black, charcoal or dark brown with red patches or stripes.

Pupils are circular in bright light.

Toes have no claws at the tips.

Banded Rubber Frog *Phrynomantis bifasciatus*
50–65 mm *Above:* Shiny black or dark grey with **two broad red-dish stripes from the snout along the sides and a large spot on the rump.** *Below:* Grey, covered with many white spots. *Limbs:* Legs banded with red. *Habitat:* Savanna pans. Calls from partly concealed positions on the banks. *Call:* Long, melodious two-second trills every five seconds. CD

Marbled Rubber Frog *Phrynomantis annectens*
30–40 mm. *Above:* Dark brown, covered with **bold, irregular-shaped reddish spots.** Body flattened and held close to the ground. *Below:* Smooth, plain pinkish skin. Male throat dark. *Limbs:* Legs spotted. Toes slightly bulbous at the tips. *Habitat:* Arid, rocky, areas where there are temporary pools. Calls from rock crevasses several metres from water. *Call:* Long, harsh insect-like trill sustained for several seconds.

Spotted Rubber Frog *Phrynomantis affinis*
50–60 mm. Known only from a few specimens. *Above:* Dark brown with **red spots arranged in two parallel rows.** Body flat-tened and held close to the ground. *Below:* Smooth. *Limbs:* Legs spotted. Toes have no bulbs at the tips. *Habitat:* No field informa-tion available but collection sites indicate sandy or rocky country in dry savanna. *Call:* not known.

Banded Rubber Frog

Marbled Rubber Frog

Spotted Rubber Frog

● *Banded Rubber Frog*

Marbled Rubber Frog ●
Spotted Rubber Frog ●

Frogs and frogging in Southern Africa

GROUP 3

GHOST FROGS

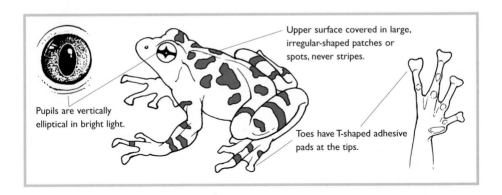

Upper surface covered in large, irregular-shaped patches or spots, never stripes.

Pupils are vertically elliptical in bright light.

Toes have T-shaped adhesive pads at the tips.

Table Mountain Ghost Frog *Heleophryne rosei*
45–60 mm. *Above:* Green with reddish mottling or patches. No dark horizontal stripe across the eye. *Below:* Granular white skin on belly. *Limbs:* Banded above; pink below. Fingers have large, T-shaped tips. *Habitat:* **Forest streams only on Table Mountain.** Calls from stream banks. *Call:* Percussive ringing notes, about two per second.

Cape Ghost Frog *Heleophryne purcelli*
40–50 mm. *Above:* Green or brown with large irregular, well-defined brick-red patches. A dark horizontal stripe runs through the eye. *Below:* Granular white skin on belly. *Limbs:* Broadly banded above; fleshy-orange below. *Habitat:* Found in **streams in fynbos and forests in mountains of the Western Cape region.** *Call:* Clear, high-pitched ringing note, one per second. CD

Table Mountain Ghost Frog

Hewitt's Ghost Frog *Heleophryne hewitti*
35–45 mm. *Above:* Light brown with numerous, irregular dark patches interspersed with small flecks. A dark horizontal stripe runs through the eye. *Below:* Granular white skin on belly. *Limbs:* Banded above, flesh-coloured below. *Habitat:* **Mountain streams in fynbos in the Elandsberg range.** *Call:* Eight to ten short whistles a second or two apart.

Southern Ghost Frog *Heleophryne regis*
35–45 mm. *Above:* Brown with yellow spots. A dark horizontal stripe runs through the eye. *Below:* Granular white skin on belly. *Limbs:* Plain or lightly marked above; flesh coloured below. *Habitat:* **Forest streams in the George-Knysna area.** Calls from crevasses and under stones. *Call:* Harsh creaking sound, about one per second.

Cape Ghost Frog

Rubber Frogs; Ghost Frogs

55

Natal Ghost Frog *Heleophryne natalensis*

50–60 mm. *Above:* Dark brown with greenish-yellow spots or marbling. No dark horizontal stripe across the eye. *Below:* Granular white skin on belly, sometimes with off-white patches. *Limbs:* Banded above, reddish-blown below. *Habitat:* **Forest streams along the eastern South African escarpment.** *Call:* Gentle, clear, repetitive whistle – two per second. CD

- Table Mountain Ghost Frog
- Cape Ghost Frog
- Southern Ghost Frog
- Hewitt's Ghost Frog
- Natal Ghost Frog

Natal Ghost Frog

Southern Ghost Frog

Hewitt's Ghost Frog

GROUP 4

RED-LEGGED KASSINAS, LEAF-FOLDING FROGS AND TREE FROGS

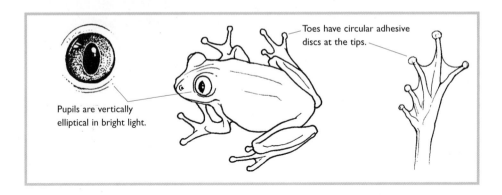

Pupils are vertically elliptical in bright light.

Toes have circular adhesive discs at the tips.

Red-legged Kassina *Kassina maculata*
60–70 mm. *Above:* Tan with large brown patches with pale outline. *Below:* Granular white. The male vocal sac is covered by an oval disc under the throat. *Limbs:* Banded above, **scarlet colouring in the groin.** *Habitat:* Lowveld savanna pans. Calls while holding onto emergent weeds in deep water. *Call:* Incessant quacking – one per second. CD

Greater Leaf-folding Frog *Afrixalus fornasinii*
30–40 mm. *Above:* A broad, brown centre stripe coming to a point between the eyes. Dark flanks. The body is **covered with white specks** and asperities. *Below:* Granular and cream. Male has a yellow disc under the throat. *Limbs:* The upper leg has dark and light longitudinal stripes. *Habitat:* Savanna pans. Calls from reeds emerging from the water. Retreats into the leaf axils of banana trees or similar plants. *Call:* A rapid series of percussive 'shots' – about ten per second. CD

Red-legged Kassina

● *Red-legged Kassina*

● *Greater Leaf-folding Frog*

Greater Leaf-folding Frog

DWARF LEAF-FOLDING FROGS

Five similar species with different calls and distribution ranges: 20–22 mm. *Above:* Yellow, sometimes with asperities and brown stripes. Flanks darker than the back. *Below:* Cream. Male has a yellow disc under the throat. *Limbs:* Legs with darker markings usually matching the flanks. *Habitat:* Savanna pans with grassy shallows.

Knysna Leaf-folding Frog

Knysna Leaf-folding Frog *Afrixalus knysnae*
Above: Faintly dotted stripes on the back. Flanks brown with white specks. **Male is evenly covered with black asperities.** *Call:* A soft, protracted 'greeee' sustained for 15–20 seconds.

Natal Leaf-folding Frog *Afrixalus spinifrons*
Above: Broad, tan centre stripe, pointed at the front. **Bulbous snout is densely covered with dark asperities.** *Call:* A short 'zip' followed by a protracted buzzing.

Natal Leaf-folding Frog

Delicate Leaf-folding Frog *Afrixalus delicatus*
Above: **A pair of faint stripes or spots on the back.** Asperities are inconspicuous. Flanks brown with white specks. *Call:* A short 'zip' followed by several seconds of rapid, high-pitched tapping at about 15 pulses per second. CD

Snoring Leaf-folding Frog *Afrixalus crotalus*
Above: Indistinguishable from the Delicate Leaf-folding Frog. *Call:* A series of clicks at about seven per second.

Delicate Leaf-folding Frog

Golden Leaf-folding Frog *Afrixalus aureus*
Above: **A pair of brown spots on the rump.** Flanks brown with white specks. *Call:* An indistinct chuckle and a quick, repeated zip or buzz. CD

● *Knysna Leaf-folding Frog*
● *Natal Leaf-folding Frog*
● *Delicate Leaf-folding Frog*

● *Snoring Leaf-folding Frog*
● *Golden Leaf-folding Frog*

Golden Leaf-folding Frog

Long-toed Tree Frog *Leptopelis xenodactylus*

50–55 mm. *Above:* Plain leaf green. *Below:* Granular white. *Limbs:* Long toes, small terminal discs. *Habitat:* **Tree-less marshland in grassland of the Drakensberg foothills.** Calls from among grass tussocks. *Call:* Short, deep croaks once or twice at long intervals.

Forest Tree Frog *Leptopelis natalensis*

45–60 mm. *Above:* Plain leaf-green or cream. Juveniles brown with green patches. *Below:* Granular white. *Limbs:* Plain, juveniles barred above. *Habitat:* Forest and coastal bush near streams. Calls from forest trees and shrubs near water. *Call:* A loud 'yack', often preceded by a soft buzzing. CD

Long-toed Tree Frog

BROWN TREE FROGS

Four similar species with overlapping distribution ranges: 50–60 mm. *Above:* Tan with **distinct brown pattern**. Juveniles under 40 mm, plain green. *Below:* Granular white. *Limbs:* Lightly patterned above. Hind feet have a digging tubercle on the heel similar to frogs in groups 8 and 9.

Brown-backed Tree Frog *Leptopelis mossambicus*

Above: **Distinct horseshoe pattern.** *Habitat:* Open woodland in savanna pans. Calls from adjacent trees and burrows into the sand by day. *Call:* A loud double 'yack-yack', often preceded by a soft buzzing. CD

Forest Tree Frog

Spotted Tree Frog *Leptopelis flavomaculatus*

Outer fingers of the forelimb are webbed. *Habitat:* Forests.

Bocage's Tree Frog *Leptopelis bocagii*

No adhesive discs on the toes. (*See* illustration and full description under Group 9, page 71.)

Silver Tree Frog *Leptopelis argenteus*

A dark triangular patch between the eyes and a pair of dark stripes down the back. Large adhesive discs on the toes. No webbing between fingers.

● *Long-toed Tree Frog*
● *Forest Tree Frog*

Brown-backed Tree Frog ●

● *Spotted Tree Frog*
  and Silver Tree Frog
● *Bocage's Tree Frog*

Brown-backed Tree Frog

GROUP 5

SHOVEL-NOSED FROGS

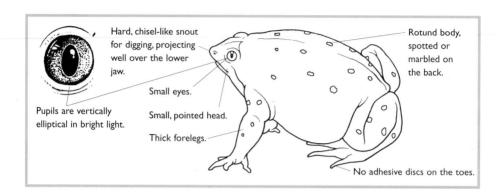

Hard, chisel-like snout for digging, projecting well over the lower jaw.

Small eyes.

Pupils are vertically elliptical in bright light.

Small, pointed head.

Thick forelegs.

Rotund body, spotted or marbled on the back.

No adhesive discs on the toes.

Spotted Shovel-nosed Frog *Hemisus guttatus*
55–80 mm. *Above:* Brown with **yellow spots**. Skin fold behind head. *Below:* Smooth off-white. Male has a dark throat. *Limbs:* Spotted. *Habitat:* Muddy banks of coastal savanna pans. Seldom found above ground. Calls from within the burrow. *Call:* Extended insect-like trills at long intervals, especially during rain.

Mottled Shovel-nosed Frog *Hemisus marmoratus*
35–45 mm. *Above:* **Mottled grey-brown with yellow.** *Below:* Smooth pinkish-white. Male has a dark throat. *Limbs:* Mottled and usually paler than the body. *Habitat:* Muddy banks of pans and slow-moving streams in savanna woodland. Calls from the mouth of burrows. *Call:* Incessant buzzing similar to that of a mole cricket. CD

A third species, the **Guinea Shovel-nosed Frog**, *Hemisus guineensis*, occurs in Zimbabwe and Botswana. It is thought to hybridize with the Mottled Shovel-nosed Frog and distribution and identification is uncertain. Specimens usually have a thin white line down the spine.

Spotted Shovel-nosed Frog

Mottled Shovel-nosed Frog

● *Spotted Shovel-nosed Frog*

Mottled Shovel-nosed ● *Frog*

GROUP 6

RATTLING FROGS AND KASSINAS

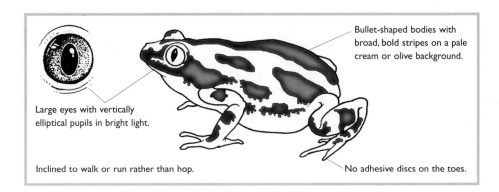

Bullet-shaped bodies with broad, bold stripes on a pale cream or olive background.

Large eyes with vertically elliptical pupils in bright light.

Inclined to walk or run rather than hop.

No adhesive discs on the toes.

Rattling Frog *Semnodactylus wealii*
35–45 mm. *Above:* Cream with dark stripes down back and sides, **each stripe divided longitudinally, showing pale background colour along the centre.** *Below:* Belly white and **coarsely granular.** The vocal sac under the male throat is covered by a dark oval disc. *Limbs:* **Yellow hands and feet.** *Habitat:* Vleis and inundated grassland. Calls from thick vegetation in shallow water. *Call:* A course, loud rattle for half a second. CD

Bubbling Kassina *Kassina senegalensis*
30–50 mm. *Above:* Cream to olive with **solid wide dark stripe down the centre of the back** and broken stripes down the sides and flanks. *Below:* **Belly smooth,** white. The vocal sac under the male throat is covered by a dark oval disc. *Limbs:* **Whitish hands and feet.** *Habitat:* Vleis in grassland. Males start calling in the grassland in mid-afternoon and move to the water's edge as night approaches. *Call:* A clear, liquid 'quoip' every few seconds. CD

Rattling Frog

● *Rattling Frog*

● *Bubbling Kassina*

Bubbling Kassina

REED FROGS, FOAM NEST FROGS AND KLOOF FROGS

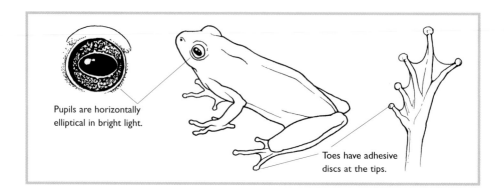

Pupils are horizontally elliptical in bright light.

Toes have adhesive discs at the tips.

Arum Lily Reed Frog *Hyperolius horstocki*

35–40 mm. *Above:* Putty-coloured. **A pale line under-scored with minute spots** runs from the snout along the flanks. *Below:* Creamy white granular skin. Males have an orange throat. *Limbs:* **Orange inner limbs and webbing.** *Habitat:* Sedges and lilies around pans in fynbos. Often occupies arum lily flowers to ambush visiting insects. *Call:* A harsh nasal bleat every half-second. CD

Yellow-striped Reed Frog *Hyperolius semidiscus*

30–35 mm. *Above:* Green or brown. **Yellow stripes with thin black borders** along the flanks, sometimes extending to the snout. *Below:* Cream or yellow granular skin. Males have a dark yellow throat. *Limbs:* **Orange or yellow inner limbs.** *Habitat:* Calls from reeds at the edges of grassland rivers and pans. *Call:* A harsh creak interspersed with longer, vibrating croaks. CD

Arum Lily Reed Frog

Arum Lily Reed Frog

Yellow-striped Reed Frog

Yellow-striped Reed Frog

Pickersgill's Reed Frog *Hyperolius pickersgilli*

20–25 mm. *Above:* Males are brown, often stippled with black. Females are opaque green. Yellow stripes bordered with black run from snout to rear but are less obvious in females. *Below:* Off-white and smooth-skinned. Males have a yellow throat. *Limbs:* **Inner limbs are flesh-coloured.** *Habitat:* Thick reeds around coastal pans. Secretive and seldom seen. *Call:* Soft cricket-like chirp at irregular intervals.

Pickersgill's Reed Frog (male)

Argus Reed Frog *Hyperolius argus*

30–35 mm. *Above:* Green or brown with **yellow stripes with heavy black border** running from snout to the eyes in females, extending onto flanks as stripes or rows of dots in males. *Below:* White or yellow with a granular skin in males, smooth and translucent in females. Males have a granular, yellow throat. *Limbs:* Inner limbs are brown or orange. *Habitat:* Lowveld pans. Calls from reeds or floating vegetation. *Call:* Rapidly repeated clucks, four per second. CD

Pickersgill's Reed Frog (female)

Long Reed Frog *Hyperolius nasutus* (possibly *H. poweri*)

20–25 mm. *Above:* Males are translucent green or brown with **silvery-white stripes** from snout to rear along flanks. Females have no stripes. Body is slender and **snout is sharply pointed.** *Below:* Silvery white and smooth. Males have a yellow throat. *Limbs:* Inner limbs are translucent green. *Habitat:* The South African population is widely separated from others to the north. Calls from inundated grassy banks and reed-beds around pans. *Call:* A harsh, acute chirp, about one per second.

Argus Reed Frog (male)

 Pickersgill's Reed Frog

 Argus Reed Frog ●

 ● Long Reed Frog

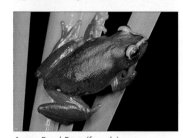

Argus Reed Frog (female)

Long Reed Frog (female)

Long Reed Frog (male)

Painted Reed Frog *Hyperolius marmoratus*

25–35 mm. *Above:* Different colour forms are dominant in differ-ent parts of the range and some are considered to be subspecies. However, one form generally runs into the next, so the subspecies labels can be confusing. A plain brown form is found throughout the range and may be confused with the Arum Lily Frog where the two species overlap. Otherwise **no patterns of the painted reed frog are the same as other species in this group.** *Below:* White or pink granular skin. Males have a grey throat, sometimes with orange spots. *Limbs:* **Red inner limbs and webbing.** *Habitat:* Savanna pans. Large choruses call from reeds near water. By day they rest in the canopy of nearby trees. *Call:* Short, loud piercing whistles, about one per second. CD

Painted Reed Frog

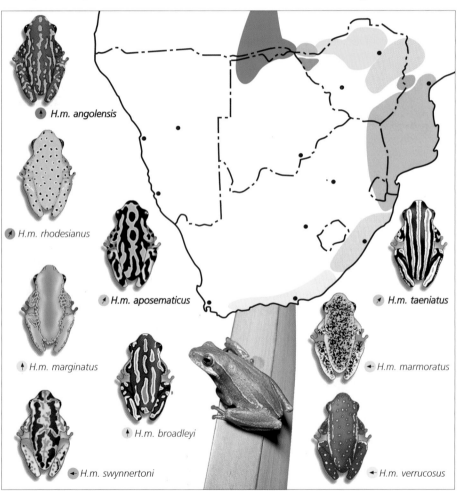

H.m. angolensis

H.m. rhodesianus

H.m. aposematicus

H.m. taeniatus

H.m. marginatus

H.m. marmoratus

H.m. broadleyi

H.m. swynnertoni

H.m. verrucosus

Painted Reed Frogs showing dominant colour forms (sub-species) in different localities. The brown form is common to all populations.

Waterlily Reed Frog *Hyperolius pusillus*

18–20 mm. *Above:* Translucent green, sometimes with stipples or very indistinct stripes. **Blunt snout.** *Below:* **Smooth and whitish or transparent.** Males have a yellow throat. *Limbs:* Translucent green inner limbs. *Habitat:* Lowveld pans. Calls from waterlily pads or other floating vegetation among reed-beds. *Call:* A blurred, high-pitched tick, about three every two seconds. CD

Tinker Reed Frog *Hyperolius tuberilinguis*

30–35 mm. *Above:* **Plain opaque green, yellow or brown.** *Below:* Cream-coloured granular skin. Males have a yellow throat. *Limbs:* Orange or yellow inner limbs and webbing. *Habitat:* Lowveld pans. Calls from concealed positions in reeds. *Call:* Two rapid staccato taps in less than a second (or occasionally a series of several taps) with long intervals in between. CD

Foam Nest Frog *Chiromantis xerampelina*

50–90 mm. *Above:* **Rough grey or tan**, sometimes with indistinct spots and markings. Becomes almost white in sunlight. *Below:* Pinkish-grey granular skin with a speckled throat. *Limbs:* Long and pliant. **Fingers of the foreleg are arranged in opposing pairs for gripping.** *Habitat:* Savanna pans. Calls and nests in trees overhanging water. *Call:* Soft, discordant croaks. CD

Kloof Frog *Natalobatrachus bonebergi*

30–35 mm. *Above:* Grey-brown with a pale central stripe of variable colour. There is often a narrow stripe within a broader one. The snout is sharply pointed with a pale triangle on top. *Below:* Off-white with dark flecks. *Limbs:* Toe tips are T-shaped. *Habitat:* Breeds in slow-moving sections of forest streams. Calls from rock shelves. *Call:* A very soft click at irregular intervals.

Waterlily Reed Frog

Tinker Reed Frog

Foam Nest Frog

● *Waterlily Reed Frog*

Tinker Reed Frog ●

● *Foam Nest Frog*

● *Kloof Frog*

Kloof Frog

65

Reed Frogs, Foam Nest Frogs and Kloof Frogs

GROUP 8

RAIN FROGS

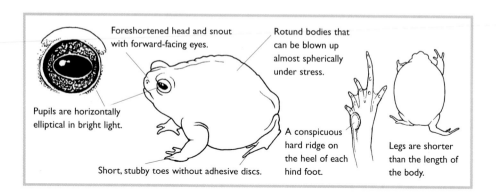

Foreshortened head and snout with forward-facing eyes.

Rotund bodies that can be blown up almost spherically under stress.

Pupils are horizontally elliptical in bright light.

A conspicuous hard ridge on the heel of each hind foot.

Legs are shorter than the length of the body.

Short, stubby toes without adhesive discs.

Cape Rain Frog *Breviceps gibbosus*

50–60 mm. *Above:* Brown with cream patches down the centre of the back, occasionally fused together. **Skin rough and granular.** *Below:* Rough skinned, mottled brown on cream. Throat of male granular. *Limbs:* Mottled. *Habitat:* Burrows near bushes or logs in fynbos. *Call:* A harsh squawk of about half a second, repeated irregularly. CD

Cape Mountain Rain Frog *Breviceps montanus*

25–30mm. **Above: Dark brown with light patches fused into a scalloped band with ridged edges down the back.** Skin rough-textured and leathery. *Below:* Light brown with many dark flecks. Throat of male dark. *Limbs:* Same colour as body. *Habitat:* Stony, scrub-covered hillsides in fynbos. Calls from among outcrops of stones. *Call:* A short series of brief whistles.

Cape Rain Frog

● *Cape Rain Frog*

● *Cape Mountain Rain Frog*

Cape Mountain Rain Frog

x

Sand Rain Frog *Breviceps rosei*

30–40 mm. *Above:* Dark grey or brown with a pale grey scalloped band down the back and, usually, a thin pale line down the spine. Orange colouring is often present. Skin slightly granular. **Eyes appear to be cast downwards.** *Below:* Pale grey-brown with a few dark flecks. Throat of male dark. *Limbs:* Same colour as body. *Habitat:* Sandy soils in dunes, flats and hillsides in fynbos. Calls from concealed positions among bushes. *Call:* Continuous very quick cheeps.

Sand Rain Frog

Strawberry Rain Frog *Breviceps acutirostris*

35–40 mm. *Above:* Reddish or pink, densely covered in black granules that almost hide the red skin in the centre of the back. *Below:* **Plum-coloured with many white spots.** Throat granular. *Limbs:* Very dark with small white spots. *Habitat:* Forest floor and adjacent fynbos. Calls from among the leaf litter. *Call:* A burred, rapidly repeated whistle.

Strawberry Rain Frog

Plain Rain Frog *Breviceps fuscus*

40–50 mm. *Above:* Uniform brown or charcoal, covered in small pointed granules. *Below:* **Plain purplish-brown.** Throat of male granular. *Limbs:* Blackish. *Habitat:* Forest floor and adjacent fynbos. *Call:* A quick chirrup repeated at about two calls every three seconds.

Namaqua Rain Frog *Breviceps namaquensis*

40–50 mm. *Above:* Brown with cream patches on the back and flanks, occasionally fused together. Skin covered with small granules. **Eyes large with dark 'mask' line behind the eye.** *Below:* White with translucent patches on the belly. Male throat granular and dark around the jaw line. *Limbs:* Hands have rough tubercles under the fingers. *Habitat:* Scrub-covered rocky outcrops in semi-desert. *Call:* Unknown.

Plain Rain Frog

● *Sand Rain Frog*

Strawberry Rain Frog ●

● *Plain Rain Frog*

Namaqua Rain Frog ●

Namaqua Rain Frog

Rain Frogs

67

Desert Rain Frog *Breviceps macrops*

40–50 mm. *Above:* Smooth yellowish cream with brown mottling forming an 'M' pattern behind the eyes. **Eyes very large (no 'mask' as in the Namaqua Rain Frog).** *Below:* Very thin, vascular, translucent skin on belly. Pure white throat and chest. Throat of male deeply wrinkled. *Limbs:* Hands and feet white, **smooth, thickly webbed and paddle-like.** *Habitat:* Desert and coastal sand dunes. *Call:* A long, clear whistle. Squeals when handled.

Plaintive Rain Frog *Breviceps verrucosus*

45–55 mm. *Above:* Dark brown or mottled with a paler region between parallel ridges of skin down the back. Skin slightly granular. The **head protrudes slightly from the body,** more than in other rain frogs. *Below:* Granular off-white with dark mottling or flecks. Throat of male dark. *Limbs:* Same colour as body. *Habitat:* Forests and adjacent grassland. *Call:* A mournful, protracted whistle about once every three seconds, especially in mist or soft rain. CD

A very similar species, the **Spotted Rain Frog** *Breviceps maculatus*, occurs in the same area and cannot be distinguished in the field.

Desert Rain Frog

Transvaal Forest Rain Frog *Breviceps sylvestris*

40–50 mm. *Above:* Dark grey or brown with **paler patches between parallel ridges of skin down the length of the back.** Skin slightly granular. *Below:* Mottled brown on yellow or white. Throat of male dark. *Limbs:* Same colour as body. *Habitat:* Forests and adjacent fringes. Calls from among leaf litter or grass tufts. *Call:* Continuous slow, burred whistles every half a second during rain.

Plaintive Rain Frog

 ● *Desert Rain Frog*

Plaintive Rain Frog ●
Transvaal Forest ●
Rain Frog

Transvaal Forest Rain Frog

Frogs and frogging in Southern Africa

Bushveld Rain Frog *Breviceps adspersus*

40–50 mm. *Above:* Mottled brown with **pairs of yellow-brown patches**, with a dark border down the back. Skin rough and granular. *Below:* Smooth white, very rarely with a few dark spots. Throat of male black; throat of female mottled. *Limbs:* Whitish with mottled upper surfaces. *Habitat:* Dry bushveld savanna with sandy soils. Avoids high-rainfall escarpment slopes and plateaux. Calls from the mouth of burrows or from other sheltered positions. *Call:* Two or three burred whistles, usually triggered by the call of a neighbour. CD

A southern population is considered to be a subspecies, *Breviceps adspersus pentheri.*

Bushveld Rain Frog

Mozambique Rain Frog *Breviceps mossambicus*

40–50 mm. *Above:* Colour and pattern are variable and sometimes resemble that of the Bushveld Rain Frog but the latter differs in habitat and call. *Habitat:* Lowveld savanna **as well as escarpment slopes and upland plateaux with good rainfall**. *Call:* Short, sharp burred whistles in small dispersed choruses – higher pitched than that of the Bushveld Rain Frog.

Whistling Rain Frog *Breviceps* sp.

A newly discovered species similar to the Bushveld and Mozambique Rain Frogs; not yet formally described but distinguishable by its call. *Habitat:* **Forest and woodland**. *Call:* A long, high-pitched whistle repeated up to 30 times a minute.

Mozambique Rain Frog

Highland Rain Frog *Probreviceps rhodesianus*

30–45 mm. *Above:* Coarsely granular grey-brown with orange markings. Flanks slightly darker than the back. The **cloaca is above the rump, and is embedded in deep skin folds**. *Below:* Densely spotted, often with orange colouring. *Limbs:* The digging ridge on the foot is less pronounced than in other species in this group. *Habitat:* Mountain forest. Found under rotting logs or leaf litter. *Call:* Unknown.

● *Bushveld Rain Frog*
● *B. a. pentheri*

Mozambique Rain Frog

● *Whistling Rain Frog*

Highland Rain Frog ●

Whistling Rain Frog

Rain Frogs

GROUP 9

BULLFROGS, SHOVEL-FOOTED SQUEAKER, ORNATE FROGS AND SAND FROGS

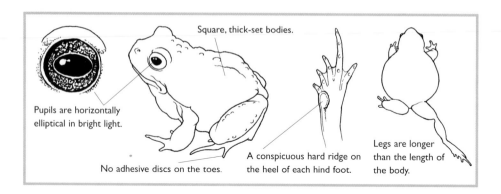

Square, thick-set bodies.

Pupils are horizontally elliptical in bright light.

No adhesive discs on the toes.

A conspicuous hard ridge on the heel of each hind foot.

Legs are longer than the length of the body.

Giant Bullfrog *Pyxicephalus adspersus*

110–200 mm. The largest southern African frog – adults may be identified by their size alone. *Above:* Olive green with ridges of whitish skin and **no patterning on the face**. The distance between the eye and the tympanum is **more than the diameter of the tympanum**. Juveniles up to about 50 mm are mottled emerald green and black. *Below:* Smooth, creamy yellow, sometimes with grey. *Limbs:* Orange in groin and armpits. Waddles, only jumps when aggressive. *Habitat:* Breeds in the shallows of temporary rain-filled depressions in grassland and dry savanna. Remains buried for most of the year. *Call:* A deep, slow bellow lasting a full second. CD

Giant Bullfrog

African Bullfrog *Pyxicephalus edulus*

90–110 mm. *Above:* Dull green and brown mottling with ridges of whitish skin and sometimes **a thin pale stripe down the back. Mottled pattern extends onto the face**, but can be indistinct. **The tympanum has a white spot.** The distance between the eye and the tympanum is **less than the diameter of the tympanum**. Juveniles up to about 50 mm are similar to the Giant Bullfrog. *Below:* Smooth, creamy yellow. *Limbs:* Not brightly coloured in groin and armpits. *Habitat:* Breeds in savanna pans. Remains buried in sandy soil for most of the year. *Call:* A short, low-pitched yap at irregular intervals. CD

Giant Bullfrog (juvenile)

Giant Bullfrog

African Bullfrog ●

African Bullfrog

Frogs and frogging in Southern Africa

Shovel-footed Squeaker *Arthroleptis stenodactylus*

35–40 mm. *Above:* Brown or grey with two or three linked diamond shapes (often indistinct or misshapen) on the back. **The top of the snout is paler than the body.** *Below:* Granular white skin with grey flecks. *Limbs:* Third finger of each hand is elongated. *Habitat:* Breeds on the sandy floor of coastal dune forest. Remains concealed among the leaf litter while calling. *Call:* Short, high-pitched chirps at the rate of about two or three per second.

Shovel-footed Squeaker

Ornate Frog *Hildebrandtia ornata*

55–65 mm. *Above:* Variations of green, black and golden brown stripes or patches on the back and flanks. *Below:* Smooth and white. The throat area is dark with **two white, Y-shapes.** Males have a pair of vocal sacs tucked into pouches on either side of the jaw. *Limbs:* Banded black and green or brown. *Habitat:* Breeds in shallow water at the edges of pans. *Call:* A long, nasal squawk about once every two seconds. CD

Bocage's Tree Frog *Leptopelis bocagii*

50–60 mm. Very similar to the Brown-Backed Tree Frog (Group 4) but does not have expanded discs on the toes. It does not climb trees. *Above:* Tan with **distinct brown horseshoe pattern.** There is sometimes a dark bar between the eyes. *Below:* Granular white. *Limbs:* Digging tubercle on hind feet. *Habitat:* Sandy areas in savanna. Calls from burrows. *Call:* A slow, low-pitched 'cluck'.

Ornate Frog

● *Shovel-footed Squeaker*

Ornate Frog ●

● *Bocage's Tree Frog*

Bocage's Tree Frog

SAND FROGS

Five similar species: 45–50 mm. *Above:* Stockily built. Wart-like elevations and irregular light and dark brown mottling and spots on the back. A pale glandular ridge or series of elevations runs from the corner of the jaw to the top of the arm. *Below:* Smooth and white with grey under the jaw, covering the throat in males.

Tremolo Sand Frog

Tremolo Sand Frog *Tomopterna cryptotus*

Above: The glandular ridge behind the jaw is continuous. There is an ochre or pale-coloured patch between the shoulders, a narrow stripe down the spine and two less distinct stripes along the flanks. *Limbs:* The tubercles on the hand are **round and uniform.** *Habitat:* Temporary rain pools, pans and vleis in savanna and grassland. Calls from exposed positions on the bank. *Call:* A rapid series of short, clear, high-pitched notes repeated at about ten per second. CD

Cape Sand Frog *Tomopterna delalandii*

Above: The glands behind the jaw form a **discontinuous row of lumps.** There is a pale grey patch between the shoulders, and a narrow stripe down the spine. *Limbs:* The tubercles on the hand are round and uniform. *Habitat:* Edges of freshwater lagoons and vleis in fynbos sometimes close to the sea. Calls from concealed positions among the vegetation. *Call:* Short, double, ringing notes at about six per second. CD

Cape Sand Frog

Tandy's Sand Frog *Tomopterna tandyi*

Indistinguishable from the Cape and the Tremolo Sand Frogs except by genetic tests in the laboratory. *Call:* Short, ringing notes at about eight per second.

Knocking Sand Frog *Tomopterna krugerensis*

Above: The patch between the shoulders is indistinct. There is seldom a line down the spine or on the flanks. Tubercles on the hand are **split into two halves.** *Call:* A wooden knocking sound at a rate of about four per second. CD

Beaded Sand Frog *Tomopterna tuberculosa*

Above: Dark grey spots or irregular markings on the back are **clearly outlined by a border of raised tubercles.** *Habitat:* Breeds in shallow pools in open savanna. *Call:* Not known.

Tremolo Sand Frog
Cape Sand Frog ◉
Tandy's Sand Frog ◉
Knocking Sand Frog ◉
Beaded Sand Frog ➔

Knocking Sand Frog

Natal Sand Frog *Tomopterna natalensis*

Above: Mottled grey or brown. The skin is leathery with two raised spots either side of the spine. **Two glandular ridges, one from the jaw and the other from the eye converge behind the tympanum.** *Limbs:* The tubercles on the hand are round and uniform. *Habitat:* Shallow seepages in grassland or the banks of streams and vleis. Calls from positions with minimal cover. *Call:* A gradual build up of accelerating croaks followed by a series of high-pitched yelps at about three per second. CD

Russet-backed Sand Frog *Tomopterna marmorata*

Above: Mottled russet with a large pale patch between the shoulders and no stripes down the spine or flanks. The skin is leathery with few wart-like elevations. **The glandular ridge behind the jaw is inconspicuous.** *Limbs:* The tubercles on the hand are round and uniform. *Habitat:* Sandbanks and rocks along quiet reaches of savanna rivers and streams. Calls from exposed positions on the banks. *Call:* Clear, piping notes repeated at a rate of about five per second, usually in choruses. CD

Natal Sand Frog

● *Natal Sand Frog*

Russet-backed ●
Sand Frog

Russet-backed Sand Frog

73

Bullfrogs, Shovel-footed Squeaker, Ornate Frogs and Sand Frogs

GROUP 10

TOADS AND SQUEAKERS

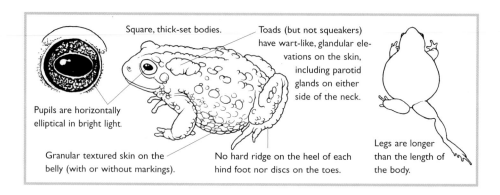

Square, thick-set bodies.

Toads (but not squeakers) have wart-like, glandular elevations on the skin, including parotid glands on either side of the neck.

Pupils are horizontally elliptical in bright light.

Granular textured skin on the belly (with or without markings).

No hard ridge on the heel of each hind foot nor discs on the toes.

Legs are longer than the length of the body.

Sand Toad *Bufo angusticeps*
Up to 60 mm. *Above:* Pairs of irregular-shaped dark brown patches on either side of a narrow stripe down the spine, from snout to rump. *Head pattern:* **One pair of dark patches on the snout and another behind the eyes.** *Below:* Granular white skin but smooth on the throat. *Limbs:* **Tops of feet are yellow.** *Habitat:* Fynbos. Breeds in temporary, rain-filled depressions. *Call:* Relatively soft nasal bray of about half a second; long intervals in between each call.

Sand Toad

Amatola Toad *Bufo amatolicus*
Less than 35 mm. *Above:* Dark patches almost obscured against the grey-brown background. Grassland in the Amatola Mountains. Breeds in temporary, rain-filled depressions. *Call:* A brief nasal squawk at long intervals.

Amatola Toad

Raucous Toad *Bufo rangeri*
Up to 100 mm. *Above:* Pairs of dark patches on the back. Occasionally a thin line down the spine, starting from between the shoulders. *Head pattern:* **The patch behind the eyes forms a single bar across the head. No patches on the snout.** *Below:* Granular white skin. The male has a dark throat. *Limbs:* No red colouration on the inner legs as in the Guttural and Olive Toads. *Habitat:* Grassland and fynbos. Breeds in still reaches of rivers, streams and man-made ponds. Males call singly or in small groups from open positions on the banks. *Call:* Short, rasping duck-like quacks repeated at about two per second. CD

Raucous Toad

● *Sand Toad*
● *Amatola Toad*

Raucous Toad ●

Western Leopard Toad *Bufo pantherinus*
Up to 140 mm. *Above:* Pairs of red-brown patches on a cream background on the back, each **patch outlined in yellow**. A narrow yellow line down the spine. *Head pattern:* **Head and large parotid glands are topped with red.** The pair of patches behind the eyes are not fused into a bar as in the Raucous Toad. No patches (or just a small spot) on the snout. *Below:* Granular white skin. Male has a dark throat. *Limbs:* No red colouration on the inner legs as in the Guttural and Olive Toads. *Habitat:* Breeds in deep water in fynbos. Males call only in early spring (August) from concealed positions along the banks. *Call:* A loud snore lasting about a second and repeated continuously every third second.

Western Leopard Toad

Eastern Leopard Toad *Bufo pardalis*
Similar to Western Leopard Toad. *Above:* The **patches on the back are not outlined in yellow.** *Call:* A deep, almost growling snore lasting more than a full second and repeated every five seconds. CD

Eastern Leopard Toad

Guttural Toad *Bufo gutturalis*
Up to 100 mm. *Above:* Pairs of dark patches on the back. Occasionally there is a thin line down the spine, especially in young frogs. *Head pattern:* **A pair of patches on the snout and another behind the eyes leave a pale cross on the head.** *Below:* Granular white skin. The male has a dark throat. *Limbs:* **Red colouring on the inner legs.** *Habitat:* Grassland and savanna. Breeds in permanent waterholes, streams and garden ponds. Males form large choruses, calling from partly concealed positions on the banks. *Call:* A vibrant snore of about one second emitted approximately every third second. CD

Guttural Toad

Flat-backed Toad *Bufo maculatus*
Not more than 65 mm. Similar to the Guttural Toad. Parotid glands are flat and inconspicuous. **There is no red colouring on the legs.**

- ● *Western Leopard Toad*
- ● *Eastern Leopard Toad*

Guttural Toad ●

● *Flat-backed Toad*

Flat-backed Toad

Toads and Squeakers

Eastern Olive Toad *Bufo garmani*

Up to 100 mm. *Above:* Pairs of dark patches on the back. Occasionally there is a thin line down the spine, starting from behind the head. *Head pattern:* Patches behind the eyes are not fused into a bar as in the Raucous Toad. **No patches on the snout.** *Below:* Granular white skin. The male has a dark throat. *Limbs:* **Red colouring on the inner legs.** *Habitat:* Breeds in savanna pans and farm dams. Males form large choruses, calling from partly concealed positions on the banks. *Call:* A loud bray of about a third of a second emitted approximately once a second. CD

Eastern Olive Toad

Western Olive Toad *Bufo poweri*

Similar to the Eastern Olive Toad. Dark patches on the back are smaller and fewer. The parotid and other elevated skin glands are reddish. The call is about half a second in duration.

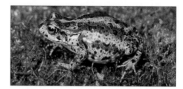

Western Olive Toad

Rose's Mountain Toad *Capensibufo rosei*

30–35 mm. *Above:* Smooth with small, blister-like elevations on the skin. Parotid glands and other elevations have a red or orange colour. **There is no tympanum.** *Below:* Granular, especially towards the rear, with grey markings. *Habitat:* Shallow pools in mountain fynbos. Large groups gather to breed in early spring but they **evidently do not call. Confined to the region south-west of Worcester.**

Rose's Mountain Toad

Tradouw Mountain Toad *Capensibufo tradouwi*

Similar to Rose's Mountain Toad. **The tympanum is visible** and this species does call. *Call:* A creaking squawk ending in a sharp squeak. Occurs north of Worcester. CD

Tradouw Mountain Toad

Karoo Toad *Bufo gariepensis*

70–90 mm. *Above:* Colouring varies from asymmetrical dark brown patches to plain khaki. Glandular elevations are rounded. *Below:* Off-white and often covered in spots, especially in young adults. *Habitat:* Breeds in temporary rain pools and streams but may forage in more arid areas. *Call:* A series of rasping squawks – about one per second at night or by day. CD

Isolated northern populations are considered to be subspecies *Bufo gariepensis nubicolus* and *B. g. inyangae*. They are smaller, less than 50 mm, with dark markings.

Karoo Toad

● *Eastern Olive Toad*
● *Western Olive Toad*

Rose's Mountain Toad ●
Tradouw Mountain Toad ●

● *Karoo Toad*
● B. g. nubicolus
● B. g. inyangae

B. g. nubicolus   B. g. inyangae

Paradise Toad *Bufo robinsoni*

60–65 mm. *Above:* Russet coloured with a number of olive-green markings, especially on glandular elevations. *Below:* Off-white with grey markings. *Limbs:* Banded with green. *Habitat:* Breeds in springs and vleis in the Richtersveld. *Call:* A subdued mewing, unlike that of any other toad species.

Southern Pygmy Toad *Bufo vertebralis*

30–35 mm. *Above:* Rough skinned, **except on the snout**, with dark markings and a pale patch between the shoulders. Parotid glands and other glandular elevations are small. *Below:* Granular white with a few black spots. *Habitat:* Breeds in temporary rocky pools on koppies in grassland. Males call from concealed positions at the water's edge. *Call:* Harsh, insect-like chirping sounds sustained continuously for long periods of time. CD

Northern Pygmy Toad *Bufo fenoulheti*

Similar to the Southern Pygmy Toad. **The rough skin extends onto the snout.** *Call:* Short, nasal bleats; about two per second.

An almost identical sub-species, *Bufo fenhoulheti hoeschi* and two very similar species, the **Beira Pygmy Toad** *Bufo beiranus* and the **Kavanga Pygmy Toad** *Bufo kavangensis* occur in isolated populations to the north. In the field they are distinguishable only because of their locality.

Red Toad *Schismaderma carens*

70–90 mm. *Above:* Brick red with **two dark spots in the middle of the back.** The skin is leathery without elevated glands. The tympanum is large. *Below:* Granular with small dark specks. Male throat is wrinkled. *Habitat:* Breeds in deep pools, farm dams and even swimming pools in savanna. Forages widely and retreats into holes in trees. Males call while floating. *Call:* A deep booming call of about one second emitted incessantly every four seconds. Large choruses call by day and night after rains. CD

H. Braack

Paradise Toad

Southern Pygmy Toad

Northern Pygmy Toad

● *Paradise Toad*

● *Southern Pygmy Toad*
● *Northern Pygmy Toad*
● *B. f. hoeschi*
◄ *Beira Pygmy Toad*
◄ *Kavanga Pygmy Toad*

● *Red Toad*

Red Toad

Toads and Squeakers

Chirinda Toad *Stephanopaedes anotis*

35–45 mm. Rarely seen. *Above:* Dark brown with **head and centre of back slightly lighter.** Parotid glands are flattened and the head and shoulders are squared off on the sides. *Below:* Whitish with irregular markings. **The cloaca points downwards and is surrounded by skin folds.** *Habitat:* Forest. Breeds in pools of water trapped between the buttress roots of trees. *Call:* Described by Fitzsimons in 1939 as 'a peculiarly plaintive medium-pitched chirrup'.

Lemaire's Toad *Bufo lemairii*

60–70 mm. *Above:* Streamlined appearance produced by pointed snout, large tympana and long toes. Overall yellowish with a pair of dark markings over the eyes and another pair on the snout, both separated by a thin pale line down the spine (often faded). *Below:* Pure white. *Habitat:* Flood-plains and large swamps. *Call:* Unknown.

Bush Squeaker *Arthroleptis wahlbergi*

25–40 mm. Those from south of the range (Port St Johns) are larger (35–40 mm) and were once considered a different species. Those from KwaZulu-Natal are under 30 mm. *Above:* Brown with **three linked diamond shapes down the centre of the back.** Top of snout is paler than the body. *Below:* Granular white with dark flecks. *Limbs:* Third finger of each hand is elongated. *Habitat:* Forests. Calls from under leaf litter. *Call:* High-pitched squeaking repeated once every second continuously during rain or mist. CD

Northern Squeaker *Arthroleptis xenodactyloides*

Similar to Bush Squeaker. Tips of toes swollen into small bulbs (but not adhesive pads).

Cave Squeaker *Arthroleptis troglodytes*

Similar to Bush Squeaker but lighter coloured. Toe tips are not expanded. Known only from caves in the Chimanimani Mountains in eastern Zimbabwe.

Chirinda Toad

A. Channing

Bush Squeaker (Port St Johns)

Bush Squeaker (KwaZulu-Natal)

● *Chirinda Toad*
● *Lemaire's Toad*

Bush Squeaker ●
Northern Squeaker ●

GROUP 11

STREAM FROGS, RIVER FROGS AND GRASS FROGS

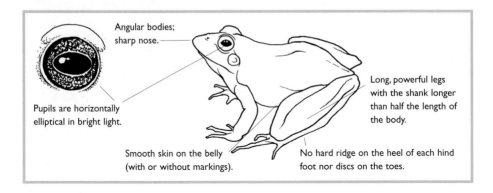

Angular bodies; sharp nose.

Pupils are horizontally elliptical in bright light.

Long, powerful legs with the shank longer than half the length of the body.

Smooth skin on the belly (with or without markings).

No hard ridge on the heel of each hind foot nor discs on the toes.

Striped Stream Frog *Strongylopus fasciatus*
35–45 mm. *Above:* Distinctive yellow and dark brown stripes with a broad, paler middle stripe. *Below:* Smooth, white. Male throat yellow. *Limbs:* **Extremely long toes extend beyond the line of the eye when the frog is at rest.** The shank is striped longitudinally. *Habitat:* Thick grass adjacent to streams, vleis, and dams with relatively permanent water. *Call:* Sharp, piercing 'pip' uttered singly or in a short burst of four or five. Choruses of males sound like twittering birds. Calling persists during autumn and early winter. CD

Striped Stream Frog

Banded Stream Frog *Strongylopus bonaspei*
Similar to the Striped Stream Frog. *Limbs:* **The legs are banded across their length.** *Habitat:* Seepage and marshy depressions in mountain fynbos. *Call:* A harsh squawk and a crackle. Males are generally widely spaced and do not form choruses. CD

Common River Frog *Afrana angolensis*
40–80 mm. *Above:* Green or brown with dark spots; often a stripe down the spine. Viewed from above, the **eyes bulge beyond the outline of the head.** *Below:* Smooth, white, often with mottling on the throat. *Limbs:* **Toes extend to the line of the armpit** when the frog is at rest. Webbing does not extend to the tip of the longest toe. *Habitat:* Grassland streams and other permanent water bodies into which they jump if disturbed. Calls from concealed or partly submerged positions at the water's edge. *Call:* Sharp rattle of about two seconds followed by a short croak, 'kikikikik-kereoow'. CD

Banded Stream Frog

● *Striped Stream Frog*
● *Banded Stream Frog*

Common River Frog ●

Common River Frog

Cape River Frog *Afrana fuscigula*

60–120 mm. Similar to the Common River Frog. *Above:* The snout is wider – viewed from directly above, **the bulge of the eyes is within the outline of the head**. *Limbs:* Feet are webbed almost to the tip of the longest toe. *Habitat:* Fynbos and grassland rivers, streams and dams. *Call:* A series of taps for about ten seconds followed by loud groan – a slower and much longer imitation of the Common River Frog call. CD

Cape River Frog

Drakensberg River Frog *Afrana dracomontana*

Indistinguishable from the Common River Frog in the field. *Habitat:* High-altitude streams in mountain grassland.

Van Dijk's River Frog *Afrana vandijki*

Similar to the Cape River Frog. *Above:* Has a **large pale patch in the centre of the back**. *Habitat:* Streams in mountain fynbos.

Drakensberg River Frog

Johnston's River Frog *Afrana johnstoni*

40–55 mm. *Above:* Greenish brown with darker spots or mottling, including a dark bar between the eyes. *Below:* White with marbling on the throat. *Limbs:* Feet are extensively webbed. *Habitat:* Mountain streams. Sits behind waterfalls and on rocks in rapids. *Call:* Not known.

Aquatic River Frog *Ameita vertebralis*

Up to 140 mm. *Above:* Brown or greenish grey with irregular spots and elevations and a pale patch in the middle of the back. The head is flattened with a wide, rounded snout. The body is slippery and held close to the ground. *Below:* White with dark vermiculations. *Limbs:* **Feet are fully webbed to the tips of all toes**. *Habitat:* Streams in high mountain grassland. Highly aquatic and can remain submerged for several hours. Tadpoles and adults are tolerant of sub-zero temperatures. *Call:* Protracted hollow tapping followed by a loud groan.

Van Dijk's River Frog

● *Cape River Frog*

Drakensberg River Frog ●
Van Dijk's River Frog ●
Johnston's River Frog ●

● *Aquatic River Frog*

Johnston's River Frog

Aquatic River Frog

Alan Channing

Clicking Stream Frog *Strongylopus grayii*

35–45 mm. *Above:* Considerable variation in colour; usually has dark spots on a grey background and may have a broad or narrow coloured stripe down the back. *Below:* Smooth, white. Male throat has a slight gold sheen. *Limbs:* **Toes extend to, but not beyond the line of the tympanum when the frog is at rest.** *Habitat:* Grassland and fynbos. Breeds in a variety of habitats – from cold, high-altitude marshland to vleis, slow-moving streams or brackish sea-side pools. *Call:* A sharp snap like the clicking of one's tongue, quickly repeated. Choruses of males give a crackling sound. CD

Isolated populations in eastern Zimbabwe are regarded as a subspecies, *Strogylopus grayii rhodesianus*.

Clicking Stream Frog

Namaqua Stream Frog *Strongylopus springbokensis*

Similar to the Clicking Stream Frog. Toes do not extend as far as the line of the tympanum when the frog is at rest. *Call:* A slow, melodious trill.

Berg Stream Frog *Strongylopus hymenopus*

45–55 mm. *Above:* **Pale grey with slightly darker grey markings in a 'V' or 'X' shape.** Covered in numerous small elevations. The head is broad with a rounded snout. *Below:* White with dark speckles on the throat. *Limbs:* Toes extend to, but not beyond the line of the tympanum when the frog is at rest. *Habitat:* Streams and seepages in mountain grassland. *Call:* A burst of chattering followed by long silences.

Namaqua Stream Frog

Alan Channing

Plain Stream Frog *Strongylopus wageri*

35–45 mm. *Above:* Plain cream, light brown or pale brick red, sometimes with dark stipples. A black mask runs through the eye with a matching stripe on the flank. *Below:* Pure white with grey around the jaw. *Limbs:* **Toes extend to, but not beyond, the line of the eye** when the frog is at rest. *Habitat:* Grassland streams in the upper escarpment. *Call:* A soft, fluttering cackle of mixed notes with brief intervals between calls.

Berg Stream Frog

● *Clicking Stream Frog*
● *S. g. rhodesianus*
● *Namaqua Stream Frog*

Berg Stream Frog ●

● *Plain Stream Frog*

Plain Stream Frog

Stream Frogs, River Frogs and Grass Frogs

Darling's Golden-backed Frog *Hylarana darlingi*

50–60 mm. *Above:* Top of head and back golden brown. **No skin ridges along the edges of the back.** Flanks deep greenish brown. *Below:* Plain white. Males have slits for a pair of vocal sacs on either side of the jaw. Juveniles are spotted. *Limbs:* Thighs mottled. *Habitat:* Marshes and pans in savanna. *Call:* Not known.

Galam Golden-backed Frog *Hylarana galamensis*

Similar to Darling's Golden-backed Frog, but larger (up to 85 mm). **A pair of skin ridges demarcate the golden-brown back from the flanks.** Males do not have vocal sac slits on the sides of the jaw.

GRASS FROGS

Nine similar species: 40–55 mm. *Above:* Ridges down the back. Sharp snout. *Below:* White or pale yellow. Males have slits for a pair of vocal sacs on either side of the jaw. *Limbs:* Legs long and powerful. Toes extend to, but not beyond, the line of the armpit when at rest. Patterns on the back of thighs are different for each species (see page 84). *Habitat:* Shallow vleis and pans in savanna and grassland.

Plain Grass Frog *Ptychadena anchietae*

40–55 mm. *Above:* **Plain brick-red** with pale triangle on snout. No light line down back nor on top of thigh. *Below:* White with pale yellow on the lower belly. *Limbs:* **Legs lighter coloured than the back.** Yellow mottling on the backs of the thighs forms one or two irregular lines not joined between the legs. *Call:* A high-pitched trill repeated at the rate of two or three per second. CD

Sharp-nosed Grass Frog *Ptychadena oxyrhynchus*

50–60 mm. *Above:* Mottled grey and brown with a pale triangle on the snout. *Limbs:* **Mottling on the back of the thighs shows no particular pattern and not joined between the legs.** *Call:* High-pitched trill; about one per second. CD

Speckled-bellied Grass Frog *Ptychadena subpunctata*

55–65 mm. *Above:* Similar to the Sharp-nosed Grass Frog, sometimes with a light line down the back. *Limbs:* **Clear dark and light stripes on the back of the thighs, running from knee to knee below the vent.**

Darling's Golden-backed Frog

Plain Grass Frog

Sharp-nosed Grass Frog

- Darling's Golden-backed Frog
- Galam Golden-backed Frog

  Plain Grass Frog ●

- Sharp-nosed Grass Frog
- Speckled-bellied Grass Frog

Striped Grass Frog *Ptychadena porosissima*

40–50 mm. *Above:* Greenish grey with darker spots and **a pale stripe from snout to rump. The outer ridges on the back are pale.** *Below:* White with pale yellow on the lower belly. *Limbs:* A thin longitudinal line along the top of the leg. **A series of irregular yellow patches on the backs of the thighs.** *Call:* Short, low-pitched rasps – about two per second. CD

Mascarene Grass Frog *Ptychadena mascareniensis*

40–50 mm. *Above:* Similar to Striped Grass Frog. *Limbs:* **Front of the thigh has a dark stripe. Backs of the thighs have continuous lines, one mottled with yellow, the other black.** *Call:* Nasal brays – two or three per second.

Striped Grass Frog

Uzungwa Grass Frog *Ptychadena uzungwensis*

40–50 mm. *Above:* Similar to Striped Grass Frog. **One pair of ridges extends from the back between the eyes onto the top of the head.** *Limbs:* Legs are crossed with numerous narrow bands and have no light longitudinal line. **Light spots on the back of thighs coalesce onto a short, irregular line not meeting between the legs.**

Broad-banded Grass Frog *Ptychadena mossambica*

40–50 mm. *Above:* Greenish grey with spots. **A broad pale stripe from snout to rump. Ridges on the back are unbroken only as far as the hump of the back.** *Below:* White with pale yellow on the belly and marbled on the throat. *Limbs:* There is a light line along the top of the leg. **Mottling on the back of the thighs is irregular with no discernable pattern.** *Habitat:* Flooded grass around savanna pans and vleis. Males call from concealed positions within grass tussocks. *Call:* Harsh nasal quacking repeated at the rate of two per second. CD

Mascarene Grass Frog

Dwarf Grass Frog *Ptychadena taenioscelis*

30–40 mm. *Above:* Brown with greenish-blue areas, with or without a central stripe. The snout is dark. *Below:* Pale yellow with spots on the throat. *Limbs:* There is no light line along the top of the leg. **Two parallel lines run across the backs of the thigh – one extends from knee to knee under the vent.** *Habitat:* Flooded grass around savanna pans and vleis. Males call at the edges of the

Broad-banded Grass Frog

● *Striped Grass Frog*

Mascarene Grass Frog ●
Uzungwa Grass Frog ●

● *Broad-banded Grass Frog*

Dwarf Grass Frog ●
Guibe's Grass Frog ●

Dwarf Grass Frog

Stream Frogs, River Frogs and Grass Frogs

water. *Call:* Short bleats repeated at the rate of one per second. The South African population is widely separated from the others to the north.

Guibe's Grass Frog *Ptychadena guibei*

30–40 mm. *Above:* Similar to Dwarf Grass Frog. *Below:* There are no spots on throat. *Limbs:* **Backs of thighs have two dark and two light stripes that do not extend across under vent.**

Comparative Grass Frog thigh patterns

Note that some variation may exist between individuals of the same species.

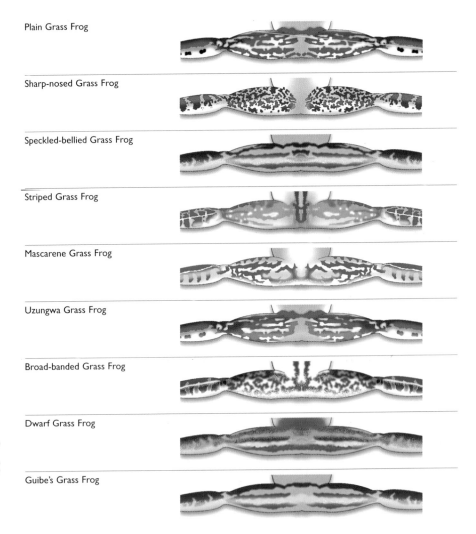

Plain Grass Frog

Sharp-nosed Grass Frog

Speckled-bellied Grass Frog

Striped Grass Frog

Mascarene Grass Frog

Uzungwa Grass Frog

Broad-banded Grass Frog

Dwarf Grass Frog

Guibe's Grass Frog

GROUP 12

CHIRPING FROGS, HOGSBACK FROG, CACOS, MICRO FROG, MARSH AND PUDDLE FROGS

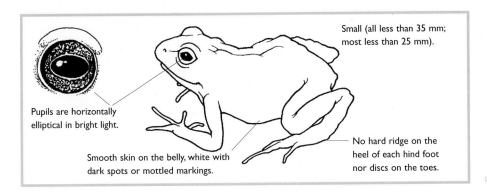

Small (all less than 35 mm; most less than 25 mm).

Pupils are horizontally elliptical in bright light.

Smooth skin on the belly, white with dark spots or mottled markings.

No hard ridge on the heel of each hind foot nor discs on the toes.

CHIRPING FROGS

Six similar species of small frogs, some indistinguishable except by laboratory genetic analysis. Isolated and restricted distribution allows them to be identified from their locality.
    20–22 mm. *Above:* Extremely variable from pale greenish brown to blue-black, sometimes with a thin line along the spine. *Below:* Variable from pure white to black. *Limbs:* No webbing between the toes. *Habitat:* Damp leaves and moss in seepages or muddy banks near mountain streams in forests, fynbos or grassland. *Call:* High-pitched chirps.

Cape Chirping Frog *Arthroleptella lightfooti*
20–22 mm. *Habitat:* Mountain streams and waterfalls in **forest in the Cape Peninsula.** *Call:* Insect-like chirps about half a second apart sustained for only short spells at a time. CD

Bainskloof Chirping Frog *Arthroleptella bicolor*
Habitat: **The mountains from Bainskloof, Du Toit's Kloof and Riviersonderend.**

Drews's Chirping Frog *Arthroleptella drewsii*
Habitat: **Mountains near Hermanus.**

Villiers's Chirping Frog *Arthroleptella villiersi*
Habitat: **Hottentots-Holland Mountains.**

Cape Chirping Frog

● *Cape Chirping Frog*
● *Bainskloof Chirping Frog*
● *Drews's Chirping Frog*
◖ *Villiers's Chirping Frog*

Natal Chirping Frog *Arthroleptella hewitti*

Habitat: **Forests of KwaZulu-Natal**. *Call:* Rapid bursts of short, piping notes repeated about four or five times per second. CD

Mist Belt Chirping Frog *Arthroleptella ngongoniensis*

Larger – up to 30 mm. *Below:* **The underside has no dark markings.** *Habitat:* Rank grass tussocks on **grassland hillside streams** in **KwaZulu-Natal**. *Call:* Three or four rapid, trilled, cricket-like calls about one second apart.

Hogsback Frog *Anhydrophryne rattrayi*

20–22 mm. *Above:* Variable from russet to almost black, sometimes with a thin line down the spine. **Snout of male is hard, sharp and colourless.** *Below:* White with dark mottling. *Limbs:* No webbing at all between toes. *Habitat:* Damp, mossy seepage near streams and especially waterfalls in the Amatola mountain forests. *Call:* Clear, melodious cheeps at the rate of about four per second. CD

Natal Chirping Frog

◈ *Natal Chirping Frog*
◈ *Mist Belt Chirping Frog*
◈ *Hogsback Frog*

Mist Belt Chirping Frog

Hogsback Frog (male and female)

CACOS AND MICRO FROG

Seven similar species of small frogs with highly variable colours. Identifiable by their calls and, in some cases, by differences in appearance and in distribution. The group is due for revision and further species may be discovered.

20–35 mm. *Above:* Various colours and patterns including browns, greens and orange. Stripes of different widths and colours are common along the spine. *Below:* White with dark spots or blotches. *Limbs:* No webbing at all between the toes.

Cape Caco *Cacosternum capense*

30–35 mm. *Above:* Cream with orange-brown speckles. There is a **bean-like glandular lump on each flank and another, double glandular lump on the rump.** No dark facial 'mask'. *Below:* White with several large dark patches on the belly and smaller ones on the throat. *Habitat:* Pans on the Cape Flats from Cape Town and Stellenbosch to Marmsbury. *Call:* Harsh creaks repeated at the rate of about two per second.

Cape Caco

Namaqua Caco *Cacosternum namaquense*

20–25 mm. *Above:* Light brown with **a white triangle over the snout and a white patch on the back.** No dark facial 'mask'. *Below:* The centre of the belly has one or **two large greenish-black patches on a white background.** Males have a grey throat. *Habitat:* Breeds in temporary pools in otherwise dry river beds in Namaqualand. *Call:* A repeated nasal bleat.

Bronze Caco *Cacosternum nanum*

20–25 mm. *Above:* Brown with **symmetrical dark flecks** and a well-defined dark facial 'mask'. *Below:* Spots are sharply defined and more prolific towards the front. *Call:* A short, creaking chirp repeated at the rate of three or four per second and interspersed with bouts of clicking. CD

Namaqua Caco

- Cape Caco
- Namaqua Caco
- Bronze Caco

Bronze Caco

Striped Caco *Cacosternum striatus*

20 mm. *Above:* Similar to Bronze Caco. Two dark lines along the sides from behind the eye to the groin. *Call:* A double, cricket-like chirp.

Poynton's Caco *Cacosternum poyntoni*

15 mm. *Above and Below:* Dark blotches on a yellow background. Known from only one specimen from Pietermaritzburg. *Call:* Unknown.

Common Caco *Cacosternum boettgeri*

20–25 mm. *Above:* Very variable colours and patterns from bright green to browns and a variety of stripes and spots. *Below:* White with randomly **scattered grey spots, slightly blurred as if under a translucent layer of skin.** Males have an orange throat without spots. *Habitat:* Marshland, inundated grass around temporary rain pools and ditches. *Call:* Explosive bursts of six to ten clicks. Choruses are almost painful to the human ear at close quarters. CD

Common Caco

Micro Frog *Microbatrachella capensis*

12–16 mm. Smallest of all southern African frogs. *Above:* Variable colours similar to the Cacos. *Below:* Black and white mottled. Male throat dark brown. **Toes are webbed for about a third of their length.** *Call:* A brisk 'tshk . . tshk' about twice a second. CD

Marsh Frog *Poyntonia paludicola*

25–30 mm. *Above:* Greyish brown with wart-like elevations and a pair of parotid-like glands behind the eyes. Often a pale, thin line along the spine. **One or two pale bands from the eye to the upper lip.** *Below:* Off-white with dark spots. *Limbs:* Toes are slightly webbed. *Habitat:* Shallow streams and marshland in mountain fynbos. *Call:* A series of up to six moderately pitched notes at a rate of about three per second.

Micro Frog

● *Striped Caco*
● *Poynton's Caco*
● *Micro Frog*

Common Caco ●

● *Marsh Frog*

Marsh Frog

PUDDLE FROGS

Four similar species of small frogs identifiable by their call and slight physical differences.

15–30 mm. *Above:* Grey or brown, often with a stripe down the back. *Below:* Smooth, off-white with flecks of grey. Males have a dark throat. *Limbs:* Toes are webbed, sometimes only slightly. *Habitat:* Vleis, grassy pans and the shallows around farm dams.

Snoring Puddle Frog *Phrynobatrachus natalensis*

25–30 mm. *Above:* Mottled with several wart-like elevations. A stripe down the back is common. *Below:* Males have a vocal sac folded into creases on either side of the jaw. *Limbs:* **Toes are webbed for almost half their length.** *Call:* A rapidly repeated nasal snoring once or twice per second. (Map, p. 88.) CD

East African Puddle Frog *Phrynobatrachus acridoides*

25–30 mm. *Above:* Similar to the Snoring Puddle Frog. There is a **pair of distinct chevron-shaped glands on the shoulders.** *Limbs:* **Toes end in very small bulbs** (not discs).

Snoring Puddle Frog

Dwarf Puddle Frog *Phrynobatrachus mababiensis*

Under 20 mm. Similar to the Snoring Puddle Frog but smaller. *Above:* The upper jaw has alternate dark and light bars. *Limbs:* Very little webbing. *Call:* A constant buzzing and ticking with no audible break when several call together.

An almost identical species, the **Small Puddle Frog** *Phrynobatrachus parvulus* from the forests of eastern Zimbabwe, is impossible to distinguish in the field.

Dwarf Puddle Frog

◉ *Snoring Puddle Frog*

◉ *East African Puddle Frog*

◉ *Dwarf Puddle Frog*

East African Puddle Frog

89

CHECKLIST OF SOUTHERN AFRICAN FROGS

Scientific name	Common Name	Habitat	Identification Group
Family: Arthroleptidae, Subfamily: Arthroleptinae			
Arthroleptis stenodactylus	Shovel-footed Squeaker	Forest	9
Arthroleptis troglodytes	Cave Squeaker	Forest	10
Arthroleptis wahlbergi	Bush Squeaker	Forest	10
Arthroleptis xenodactyloides	Northern Squeaker	Forest	10
Family: Bufonidae			
Bufo amatolicus	Amatola Toad	Grassland	10
Bufo angusticeps	Sand Toad	Fynbos	10
Bufo beiranus	Beira Toad	Savanna	10
Bufo fenoulheti	Northern Pygmy Toad	Savanna	10
Bufo gariepensis	Karoo Toad	Desert, grassland, fynbos	10
Bufo garmani	Eastern Olive Toad	Savanna	10
Bufo gutturalis	Guttural Toad	Grassland, savanna	10
Bufo kavangensis	Kavanga Pygmy Toad	Savanna	10
Bufo lemairii	Lemaire's Toad	Savanna	10
Bufo maculatus	Flat-backed Toad	Savanna	10
Bufo pantherinus	Western Leopard Toad	Fynbos	10
Bufo pardalis	Eastern Leopard Toad	Grassland, fynbos	10
Bufo poweri	Western Olive Toad	Savanna, desert	10
Bufo rangeri	Raucous Toad	Grassland, fynbos	10
Bufo robinsoni	Paradise Toad	Desert	10
Bufo vertebralis	Southern Pygmy Toad	Grassland	10
Capensibufo rosei	Rose's Mountain Toad	Fynbos	10
Capensibufo tradouwi	Tradouw Mountain Toad	Fynbos	10
Schismaderma carens	Red Toad	Savanna, grassland	10
Stephanopaedes anotis	Chirinda Toad	Forest	10
Family: Heleophrynidae			
Heleophryne hewitti	Hewitt's Ghost Frog	Fynbos	3
Heleophryne natalensis	Natal Ghost Frog	Forest	3
Heleophryne purcelli	Cape Ghost Frog	Fynbos	3
Heleophryne regis	Southern Ghost Frog	Forest	3
Heleophryne rosei	Table Mountain Ghost Frog	Forest	3
Family: Hemisotidae, Subfamily: Hemisotinae			
Hemisus guineensis	Guinea Shovel-nosed Frog	Savanna	5
Hemisus guttatus	Spotted Shovel-nosed Frog	Savanna	5
Hemisus marmoratus	Mottled Shovel-nosed Frog	Savanna	5
Family: Hyperoliidae, Subfamily: Kassininae			
Afrixalus aureus	Golden Leaf-folding Frog	Savanna	4
Afrixalus crotalus	Snoring Leaf-folding Frog	Savanna	4
Afrixalus delicatus	Delicate Leaf-folding Frog	Savanna	4
Afrixalus fornasinii	Greater Leaf-folding Frog	Savanna	4
Afrixalus knysnae	Knysna Leaf-folding Frog	Savanna, grassland, fynbos	4
Afrixalus spinifrons	Natal Leaf-folding Frog	Savanna, grassland	4
Kassina maculata	Red-legged Kassina	Savanna	4

| *Kassina senegalensis* | Bubbling Kassina | Grassland, grassland | 6 |
| *Semnodactylus wealii* | Rattling Frog | Grassland | 6 |

Family: Hyperoliidae, Subfamily: Hyperoliinae

Hyperolius argus	Argus Reed Frog	Savanna	7
Hyperolius horstocki	Arum Lily Reed Frog	Fynbos	7
Hyperolius marmoratus	Painted Reed Frog	Savanna, grassland	7
Hyperolius nasutus	Long Reed Frog	Savanna	7
Hyperolius pickersgilli	Pickersgill's Reed Frog	Savanna	7
Hyperolius pusillus	Waterlily Reed Frog	Savanna	7
Hyperolius semidiscus	Yellow-striped Reed Frog	Grassland	7
Hyperolius tuberilinguis	Tinker Reed Frog	Savanna	7

Family: Hyperoliidae, Subfamily: Leptopelinae

Leptopelis argenteus	Silver Tree Frog	Forest	4
Leptopelis bocagii	Bocage's Tree Frog	Savanna	9
Leptopelis flavomaculatus	Spotted Tree Frog	Forest	4
Leptopelis mossambicus	Brown-backed Tree Frog	Savanna	4
Leptopelis natalensis	Forest Tree Frog	Forest	4
Leptopelis xenodactylus	Long-toed Tree Frog	Grassland	4

Family: Microhylidae, Subfamily: Breviceptinae

Breviceps acutirostris	Strawberry Rain Frog	Forest	8
Breviceps adspersus	Bushveld Rain Frog	Savanna, grassland	8
Breviceps fuscus	Plain Rain Frog	Forest	8
Breviceps gibbosus	Cape Rain Frog	Fynbos	8
Breviceps macrops	Desert Rain Frog	Desert	8
Breviceps maculatus	Spotted Rain Frog	Forest, grassland	8
Breviceps montanus	Cape Mountain Rain Frog	Fynbos	8
Breviceps mossambicus	Mozambique Rain Frog	Savanna, grassland	8
Breviceps namaquensis	Namaqua Rain Frog	Desert	8
Breviceps rosei	Sand Rain Frog	Fynbos	8
Breqviceps sp.	Whistling Rain Frog	Savanna	8
Breviceps sylvestris	Transvaal Forest Rain Frog	Forest	8
Breviceps verrucosus	Plaintive Rain Frog	Forest, grassland	8
Probreviceps rhodesianus	Highland Rain Frog	Forest	8

Family: Microhylidae, Subfamily: Phrynomerinae

Phrynomantis affinis	Spotted Rubber Frog	Savanna, desert	2
Phrynomantis annectens	Marbled Rubber Frog	Desert	2
Phrynomantis bifasciatus	Banded Rubber Frog	Savanna	2

Family: Pipidae, Subfamily: Xenopodinae

Xenopus gilli	Cape Platanna	Fynbos	I
Xenopus laevis	Common Platanna	All	I
Xenopus muelleri	Tropical Platanna	Savanna	I

Family: Ranidae, Subfamily: Raninae

Afrana angolensis	Common River Frog	Grassland, savanna	II
Afrana dracomontana	Drakensberg River Frog	Grassland	II
Afrana fuscigula	Cape River Frog	Grassland, fynbos, desert	II
Afrana johnstoni	Johnston's River Frog	Grassland	II
Afrana vandijki	Van Dijk's River Frog	Fynbos	II
Ametia vertebralis	Aquatic River Frog	Grassland	II
Hildebrandtia ornata	Ornate Frog	Savanna	9

Hylarana darlingi	Darling's Golden-backed Frog	Savanna	11
Hylarana galamensis	Galam Golden-backed Frog	Savanna	11
Ptychadena anchietae	Plain Grass Frog	Savanna	11
Ptychadena guibei	Guibe's Grass Frog	Savanna	11
Ptychadena mascareniensis	Mascarene Grass Frog	Savanna	11
Ptychadena mossambica	Broad-banded Grass Frog	Savanna	11
Ptychadena oxyrhynchus	Sharp-nosed Grass Frog	Savanna	11
Ptychadena porosissima	Striped Grass Frog	Grassland, savanna	11
Ptychadena subpunctata	Speckled-bellied Grass Frog	Savanna	11
Ptychadena taenioscelis	Dwarf Grass Frog	Savanna	11
Ptychadena uzungwensis	Uzungwa Grass Frog	Savanna	11
Pyxicephalus adspersus	Giant Bullfrog	Grassland, savanna	9
Pyxicephalus edulus	African Bullfrog	Savanna	9
Strongylopus bonaspei	Banded Stream Frog	Fynbos	11
Strongylopus fasciatus	Striped Stream Frog	Grassland, fynbos	11
Strongylopus grayii	Clicking Stream Frog	Grassland, forest, fynbos	11
Strongylopus hymenopus	Berg Stream Frog	Grassland	11
Strongylopus springbokensis	Namaqua Stream Frog	Desert	11
Strongylopus wageri	Plain Stream Frog	Grassland	11
Tomopterna cryptotus	Tremolo Sand Frog	Savanna. Grassland, desert	9
Tomopterna delalandii	Cape Sand Frog	Fynbos	9
Tomopterna krugerensis	Knocking Sand Frog	Savanna	9
Tomopterna marmorata	Russet-backed Sand Frog	Savanna	9
Tomopterna natalensis	Natal Sand Frog	Grassland, savanna	9
Tomopterna tandyi	Tandy's Sand Frog	Grassland, savanna, fynbos	9
Tomopterna tuberculosa	Beaded Sand Frog	Savanna	9

Family: Ranidae, Subfamily: Petropedetinae

Anhydrophryne rattrayi	Hogsback Frog	Forest	12
Arthroleptella bicolor	Bainskloof Chirping Frog	Forest, fynbos	12
Arthroleptella drewsii	Drews's Chirping Frog	Forest, fynbos	12
Arthroleptella hewitti	Natal Chirping Frog	Forest	12
Arthroleptella lightfooti	Cape Chirping Frog	Forest, fynbos	12
Arthroleptella ngongoniensis	Mist belt Chirping Frog	Grassland	12
Arthroleptella villiersi	Villiers's Chirping Frog	Forest, fynbos	12
Cacosternum boettgeri	Common Caco	Grassland, savanna, fynbos	12
Cacosternum capense	Cape Caco	Fynbos	12
Cacosternum namaquense	Namaqua Caco	Desert	12
Cacosternum nanum	Bronze Caco	Grassland, fynbos	12
Cacosternum poyntoni	Poynton's Caco	Grassland	12
Cacosternum striatus	Striped Caco	Grassland	12
Microbatrachella capensis	Micro Frog	Fynbos	12
Natalobatrachus bonebergi	Kloof Frog	Forest	7
Phrynobatrachus acridoides	East African Puddle Frog	Savanna	12
Phrynobatrachus mababiensis	Dwarf Puddle Frog	Savanna	12
Phrynobatrachus natalensis	Snoring Puddle Frog	Grassland, savanna	12
Phrynobatrachus parvulus	Small Puddle Frog	Forest, savanna	12
Poyntonia paludicola	Marsh Frog	Fynbos	12

Family: Rhacophoridae, Subfamily: Rhacophorinae

Chiromantis xerampelina	Foam Nest Frog	Savanna	7

GLOSSARY

Afromontane forest – high, closed canopy forest growing on mountain slopes where rising moist air precipitates rainfall.

Amplexus – clasping of the female by the male while mating.

Aposematic colours – skin colouring that signals that the frog is poisonous.

Arboreal – living in trees.

Arthropods – invertebrate animals with jointed legs such as insects and spiders.

Asperities – small, sharp or rough pimple-like elevations on the skin.

Batrachian – an amphibian without a tail, i.e. all families of frogs including toads.

Biodiversity – the range of plant and animal life that makes up an ecological community.

Biome – a community of animals and plants associated with a predominant type of vegetation and adapted to a particular environment.

Call attenuation – the decline in the audibility of the call over distance, especially of the higher notes.

Cardiotoxins – poisons affecting the heart.

Cartilage – tough pliable tissue similar to bone in function.

Cloaca – the chamber into which the intestinal, urinary and reproductive systems enter, opening to the exterior through the vent or anus.

Coastal forest – closed canopy bush and scrub growing on coastal dunes.

Crepuscular – active at dawn and at dusk.

Cryptically coloured – coloured in a manner that conceals the frog in its environment.

Dambo – a wet, marshy area (Zimbabwe).

Donga – an excavation or ditch caused by erosion of soil.

Dorsum (adj. dorsal) – the back or upper surface of the body.

Explosive breeding – mating, egg-laying, hatching and metamorphosis that takes place over a short period of time to take advantage of temporary breeding sites or suitable weather.

Genus – a group of species that have a number of shared characters indicating a common evolutionary ancestry.

Granular – grainy or pebble-like surface of the skin.

Gular sac – stretchable skin under the throat that expands into a balloon when the frog calls.

Habitat – the type of locality in which an animal occurs naturally.

Inselbergs – isolated rocky outcrops.

Larynx – cartilage structure in the throat used for creating sound.

Marbled – veined or dappled skin markings resembling marble.

Metamorphosis – the transformation from tadpole to adult frog.

Monoculture – a crop of one species cultivated throughout an entire area.

Parotid glands – a pair of elongated, oval-shaped glands situated on the neck behind the eyes of most species of toads.

Quadruped – a vertebrate animal with four legs.

Quartzite – a hard, weather-resistant rock made up of quartz crystals.

Riverine forest – closed canopy woodland growing along the banks of rivers.

Shank – the tibia or shin bone – the longest section of the frog's leg.

Species – a population that breed naturally with one another and produce viable offspring.

Stippled – dotted patterning on the skin.

Taxonomy – the science of classifying animals and plants.

Terrestrial breeding – breeding where the egg and tadpole stages occur away from standing water.

Tubercle – small, rounded nodule.

Tympanum – the visible eardrum; the membrane covering the ear.

Vent – the anus or exterior opening of the urinal, digestive and reproductive tract.

Venter (adj. ventral) – the belly or lower surface of the body.

Vertebral line – a line running down the length of the spine.

Vertebrate – an animal with a spinal column.

Vermiculations – a pattern of interconnecting curved lines and markings on the skin.

Vocal sac – a chamber of elastic skin under the throat that is inflated as the male frog calls.

FURTHER READING

Carruthers, Vincent, ed. (1997), *The Wildlife of Southern Africa: A Field Guide to the Animals and Plants of the Region*. Johannesburg, Southern Book Publishers.

Channing, A, *Amphibians of Central and Southern Africa*. Cornell University Press. (In press.)

Du Preez, Louis (1996), *Field Guide and Key to the Frogs and Toads of the Free State*. Bloemfontein, University of the Free State.

Lambiris, A.J.L. (1988), *Frogs and Toads of the Natal Drakensberg*. Pietermaritzburg, University of Natal Press.

Mason, M.C. and Carruthers, V.C. (1998), *Frogs of Gauteng and North-West Province: A Beginner's Guide*. Howick, Share-Net.

Pienaar, U. De V., Passmore, N.I. and Carruthers, V.C. (1976), *The Frogs of the Kruger National Park*. Pretoria, National Parks Board.

Passmore, N.I. and Carruthers, V.C. (1995), *South African Frogs: A Complete Guide*. Revised edition. Halfway House, Southern Book Publishers and Witwatersrand University Press.

Poynton, J.C. and Broadley, D.G. (1985), *Amphibia Zambesiaca 2*. Ranidae. Ann. Natal Mus. 27, 115–181.

Poynton, J.C. (1964), *The Amphibia of Southern Africa: A Faunal Study*. Ann. Natal Mus. 17, 1–334.

Rose, Walter (1962), *The Reptiles and Amphibians of Southern Africa*. Cape Town, Maskew Miller.

Schiotz, Arne (1999), *Treefrogs of Africa*. Frankfurt am Main, Edition Chimaira.

Wager, V.A. (1986), *Frogs of South Africa: Their Fascinating Life Stories*. Johannesburg, Delta Books.

Stewart, Margaret M. (1967), *Amphibians of Malawi*. Albany, N.Y., State University of New York Press.

The Atlas of Southern African Frogs. Avian Demography Unit. University of Cape Town. (In press.)

Frogs on the 'Red Data' List

(South Africa, Lesotho and Swaziland)

CRITICALLY ENDANGERED	
Mist Belt Chirping Frog	*Arthroleptella ngongoniensis*
Hewitt's Ghost Frog	*Heleophryne hewitti*
Table Mountain Ghost Frog	*Heleophryne rosei*
Micro Frog	*Microbatrachella capensis*
ENDANGERED	
Western Leopard Toad	*Bufo pantherinus*
Long-toed Tree Frog	*Leptopelis xenodactylus*
Pickersgill's Reed Frog	*Hyperolius pickersgilli*
Kloof Frog	*Natalobatrachus bonebergi*
Cape Platanna	*Xenopus gilli*
VULNERABLE	
Rose's Mountain Toad	*Capensibufo rosei*
Cape Caco	*Cacosternum capense*
THREATENED	
Amatola Toad	*Bufo amatolicus*
Spotted Shovel-nosed Frog	*Hemisus guttatus*
Cape Rain Frog	*Breviceps gibbosus*
Desert Rain Frog	*Breviceps macrops*
Transvaal Forest Rain Frog	*Breviceps sylvestris*
Hogsback Frog	*Anhydrophryne rattrayi*
Drews's Chirping Frog	*Arthroleptella drewesii*
Lightfoot's Chirping Frog	*Arthroleptella lightfooti*
Marsh Frog	*Poyntonia paludicola*
Giant BullFrog	*Pyxicephalus adspersus*
POSSIBLY THREATENED BUT INSUFFICIENT DATA AVAILABLE	
Paradise Toad	*Bufo robinsoni*
Vandijk's River Frog	*Afrana vandijki*
Striped Caco	*Cacosternum striatum*
Namaqua Stream Frog	*Strongylopus springbokensis*

Source: South African Frog Atlas Project, Avian Demography Unit, University of Cape Town.

INDEX

List of frog calls recorded on CD

TRACK 1
Introduction

TRACK 2
Frogs in Groups 1, 2 and 3

Xenopus laevis
  Common Platanna
Phrynomantis bifasciatus
  Banded Rubber Frog
Heleophryne purcelli
  Cape Ghost Frog
Heleophryne natalensis
  Natal Ghost Frog

TRACK 3
Frogs in Group 4

Kassina maculata
  Red-legged Kassina
Afrixalus fornasinii
  Greater Leaf-folding Frog
Afrixalus delicatus
  Delicate Leaf-folding Frog
Afrixalus aureus
  Golden Leaf-folding Frog
Leptopelis mossambicus
  Brown-backed Tree Frog
Leptopelis natalensis
  Forest Tree Frog

TRACK 4
Frogs in Groups 5 and 6

Hemisus marmoratus
  Mottled Shovel-nosed Frog
Semnodactylus wealii
  Rattling Frog
Kassina senegalensis
  Bubbling Kassina

TRACK 5
Frogs in Group 7

Hyperolius horstocki
  Arum Lily Reed Frog
Hyperolius semidiscus
  Yellow-striped Reed Frog
Hyperolius argus
  Argus Reed Frog

Hyperolius marmoratus
  Painted Reed Frog
Hyperolius pusillus
  Waterlily Reed Frog
Hyperolius tuberilinguis
  Tinker Reed Frog
Chiromantis xerampelina
  Foam Nest Frog

TRACK 6
Frogs in Group 8

Breviceps gibbosus
  Cape Rain Frog
Breviceps verrucosus
  Plaintive Rain Frog
Breviceps adspersus
  Bushveld Rain Frog

TRACK 7
Frogs in Group 9

Pyxicephalus adspersus
  Giant Bullfrog
Pyxicephalus edulis
  African Bullfrog
Hildebrandtia ornata
  Ornate Frog
Tomopterna cryptotus
  Tremolo Sand Frog
Tomopterna delalandii
  Cape Sand Frog
Tomopterna krugerensis
  Knocking Sand Frog
Tomopterna natalensis
  Natal Sand Frog
Tomopterna marmorata
  Russet-backed Sand Frog

TRACK 8
Frogs in Group 10

Bufo rangeri
  Raucous Toad
Bufo pardalis
  Eastern Leopard Toad
Bufo gutturalis
  Guttural Toad
Bufo garmani
  Eastern Olive Toad

Capensibufo tradouwi
  Tradouw Mountain Toad
Bufo gariepensis
  Karoo Toad
Bufo vertebralis
  Southern Pygmy Toad
Schismaderma carens
  Red Toad
Arthroleptis wahlbergi
  Bush Squeaker

TRACK 9
Frogs in Group 11

Strongylopus fasciatus
  Striped Stream Frog
Strongylopus bonaspei
  Banded Stream Frog
Afrana angolensis
  Common River Frog
Afrana fuscigula
  Cape River Frog
Strongylopus grayii
  Clicking Stream Frog
Ptychadena anchietae
  Plain Grass Frog
Ptychadena oxyrhynchus
  Sharp-nosed Grass Frog
Ptychadena porosissima
  Striped Grass Frog
Ptychadena mossambica
  Broad-banded Grass Frog

TRACK 10
Frogs in Group 12

Arthroleptella lightfooti
  Cape Chirping Frog
Arthroleptella hewitti
  Natal Chirping Frog
Anhydrophryne rattrayi
  Hogsback Frog
Cacosternum nanum
  Bronze Caco
Cacosternum boettgeri
  Common Caco
Microbatrachella capensis
  Micro Frog
Phrynobatrachus natalensis
  Snoring Puddle Frog

Notes